THE IDEALS TREASURY OF FAITH IN AMERICA

He who looks with pride upon his history which his fathers have written by their heroic deeds, who accepts with gratitude the inheritance which they have bequeathed to him, and who highly resolves to preserve this inheritance unimpaired and to pass it on to his descendants enlarged and enriched, is a true American, be his birthplace or his percentage what it may.

—Reverend Lyman Abbott

THE IDEALS
TREASURY OF

Faith IN

AMERICA

EDITED BY PATRICIA A. PINGRY

IDEALS PUBLICATIONS
NASHVILLE, TENNESSEE

ISBN 0-8249-5858-6

Published by Ideals Publications
A division of Guideposts
535 Metroplex Drive, Suite 250
Nashville, Tennessee 37211
www.idealsbooks.com

Printed and bound in U.S.A. by RR Donnelley, Willard, Ohio

Color separations by Precision Color Graphics, Franklin, Wisconsin

Library of Congress CIP data on file

Front cover: The American Flag © by Fred Sieb/H. Armstrong Roberts.

10 9 8 7 6 5 4 3 2 1

Publisher, Patricia A. Pingry
Art Director, Eve DeGrie
Copy Editor, Melinda Rathjen
Permissions Editor, Patsy Jay

Book Design by Eve DeGrie

ACKNOWLEDGMENTS

BERLIN, IRVING. "God Bless America." Copyright © 1938, 1939 and renewed 1965, 1966 by Irving Berlin. Copyright assigned to the Trustees of the God Bless America Fund. All rights reserved. Used by permission. HAND, JUDGE LEARNED. An excerpt from *The Spirit of Liberty* by Learned Hand, edited by I. Dilliard. Copyright © 1952-1960 by Alfred A. Knopf, a division of Random House, Inc. Used by permission of the publisher. KING, MARTIN LUTHER, JR. "March on Washington Address." Copyright © 1963 by Martin Luther King, Jr., renewed 1991 by Coretta Scott King. Reprinted by arrangement with the Estate of Martin Luther King, Jr, c/o Writers House as agent for the proprietor, New York, NY. MACARTHUR, GENERAL DOUGLAS. "Duty—Honor—Country." Used by permission of the General Douglas MacArthur Foundation, Norfolk, VA. MCCAIN, JOHN. "The Lanterns of Faith" from *Faith of My Fathers* by John McCain and Mark Salter. Copyright © 1999 by the authors. Used by permission of Random House, Inc. MARSHALL, PETER. "Prayer" from *The Prayers of Peter Marsall*. Copyright © 1949–1954 by Catherine Marshall and renewed 1982. Published by Chosen Books, Fleming Revell Co. Used by permission of Baker Book House Co. STOFFEL, BETTY W. "Fourth of July." Used by permission of E. Lee Stoffel. WHITE, THEODORE H. "The American Idea." An excerpt from an original article by Theodore H. White in the *New York Times*. Copyright © 1986.

Every effort has been made to contact copyright owners of each selection printed in this book. Should errors be found, please contact the publisher.

Table of CONTENTS

THE EMBARKATION OF THE PILGRIMS by
Robert W. Weir 1803-1845. © SuperStock
(900-128903).

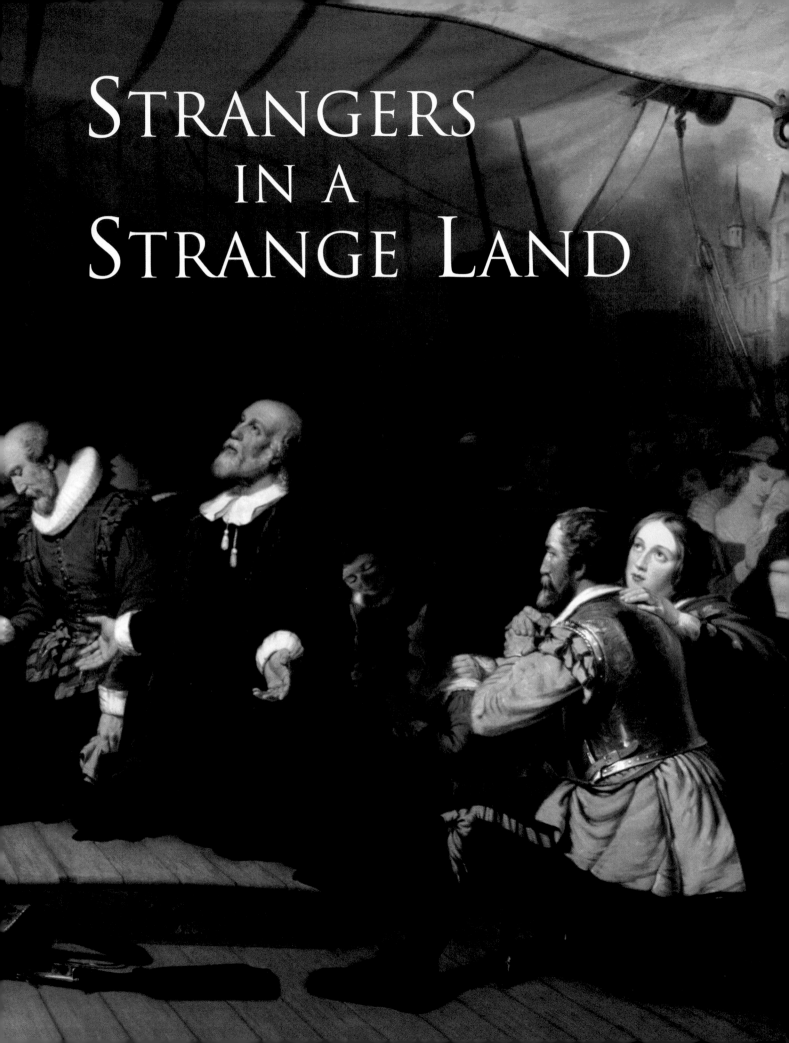

Strangers
in a
Strange Land

Note: spellings have been modernized.

It resteth I speak a word or two of the natural inhabitants, their natures and manners. . . . They are a people clothed with loose mantles made of deer skins and aprons of the same round about their middles; all else naked; of such a difference of stature only as we in England; having no edge tools or weapons of iron or steel to offend us withal, neither know they how to make any: those weapons they have are only bows made of witch hazel and arrows of reeds. . . .

They believe that there are many gods which they call Mantoac, but of different sorts and degrees; one only chief and great God, which hath been from all eternity. Who, as they affirm, when he purposed to make the world, made first other gods of a principal order to be as means and instruments to be used in the creation and government to follow. . . .

They believe also the immortality of the soul, that after this life as soon as the soul is departed from the body, according to the works it hath done, it is either carried to heaven, the habitat of the gods, there to enjoy perpetual bliss and happiness, or else to a great pit or hole, which they think to be in the furthest parts of their part of the world toward the sunset, there to burn continually, the place they call Popogusso. . . .

Many times and in every town where I came, according as I was able, I made declaration of the contents of the Bible; that therein was set forth the true and only God, and his mightie works, that therein was contained the true doctrine of salvation through Christ, with many particularities of miracles and chief points of religion, as I was able then to utter, and thought fit for the time. And although I told them the book materially and of itself was not of any such virtue, as I thought they did conceive, but only the doctrine therein contained; yet would many be glad to touch it, to embrace it, to kiss it, to hold it to their breasts and heads, and stroke over all their body with it to show their hungry desire of that knowledge which was spoken of. . . .

A BRIEFE AND TRUE REPORT OF THE NEW FOUND LAND OF VIRGINIA

Thomas Hariot, 1588

Shenandoah State Park, Virginia. © Witold Skrypczak/SuperStock (1299-970A).

8

THE IDEALS TREASURY OF FAITH IN AMERICA

THE PROMISE OF THE NEW WORLD

John Smith, 1616

Replica of the original Jamestown Settlement, Jamestown, Virginia. © W. Bertsch/H. Armstrong Roberts (KH-11310).

Who can desire more content, that hath small means; or but only his merit to advance his fortunes, then to tread and plant that ground he hath purchased by the hazard of his life? . . . What so truly suits with honor and honesty, as the discovering things unknown? erecting towns, peopling countries, informing the ignorant, reforming things unjust, teaching virtue . . . ?

We are now remaining being in good health, all our men well contented, free from mutinies, in love with one another; and as we hope in continual peace with the Indians, where we doubt not, by God's gracious assistance and the adventurers' willing minds and speedy furtherance to so honorable action, in after times to see our nation to enjoy a country not only exceeding pleasant for habitation but also very profitable for commerce in general, no doubt pleasing to almighty God, honorable to our gracious sovereign, commodious generally to the whole Kingdom.

THE MAYFLOWER COMPACT

1620

In the name of God, Amen. We whose names are underwritten, the loyal subjects of our dread sovereign Lord, King James, by the grace of God, of Great Britain, France, and Ireland king, defender of the faith, etc., having undertaken, for the glorie of God, and advancement of the Christian faith, and honour of our king and country, a voyage to plant the first colony in the Northern parts of Virginia, do by these presents solemnly and mutually in the presence of God, and one of another, covenant and combine our selves together into a civil body politick for our better ordering and preservation and furtherance of the ends aforesaid; and by virtue hearof to enact, constitute, and frame such just and equal laws, ordinances, acts, constitutions, and offices, from time to time, as shall be thought most meet and convenient for the generally good of the Colony, unto which we promise all due submission and obedience. In witness whereof we have hereunder subscribed our names at Cape Cod the 11 of November, in the year of the reign of our sovereign lord, King James, of England, France, and Ireland the eighteenth, and of Scotland the fiftie fourth. Anº: Dom. 1620.

—From Bradford's *History of Plymoth Plantation*, 1630

THE MAYFLOWER AT SEA, by Gilbert Margeson, 1852–1949, American. © Jack Novak/SuperStock (2061-546992).

12

HISTORY OF PLYMOUTH PLANTATION

William Bradford, 1620

America's treasure, Plymouth Rock, now lies protected by a permanent canopy. © R. Krubner/H. Armstrong Roberts. (KH-3373).

B eing thus arrived in a good harbor and brought safe to land, they fell upon their knees & blessed the God of heaven, who had brought them over the vast and furious ocean, and delivered them from all the perils and miseries thereof, again to set their feet on the firm and stable earth. . . .

But here I cannot but stay and make a pause, and stand half amazed at this poor people's present condition; and so I think will the reader too, when he well considers the same. Being thus passed the vast ocean, and a sea of troubles before in their preparation . . . they had now no friends to welcome them, nor inns to entertain or refresh their weather-beaten bodies, no houses or much less towns to repair to, to seek for succor. . . .

For the season, it was winter, and they that know the winters of that country know them to be sharp and violent and subject to cruel and fierce storms, dangerous to travel to known places, much more to search an unknown coast. Besides, what could they see but a hideous and desolate wilderness, full of wild beasts and wild men? And what multitudes of them there might be of them they knew not. Neither could they, as it were, go up to the top of Pisgah, to view from the wilderness a more goodly country to feed their hopes; for which way soever they turned their eyes (save upward to the heavens), they could have little solace or content in respect of any outward objects.

For summer being done, all things stand upon them with a weather-beaten face; and the whole country, full of woods and thickets, represented a wild and savage hew. . . .

What could now sustain them but the spirit of God and his grace? May not and ought not the children of these fathers rightly say: Our fathers were Englishmen which came over this great ocean and were ready to perish in the wilderness, but they cried unto the Lord, and he heard their voice, and looked on their adversity. Let them therefore praise the

14

Lord, because he is good, and his mercies endure forever. Yea, let them which have been redeemed of the Lord, show how he hath delivered them from the hand of the oppressor. When they wandered in the desert wilderness out of the way and found no city to dwell in, both hungry and thirsty, their soul was overwhelmed in them. Let them confess before the Lord his loving kindness, and his wonderful works before the sons of men. . . .

A MODELL OF CHRISTIAN CHARITY

John Winthrop, 1790

THE FIRST
THANKSGIVING 1621 by
Jean Leon Gerome
Ferris, 1863-1930.
SuperStock (900-
101850).

Thus stands the cause between God and us, we are entered into Covenant with him for this work, we have taken out a Commission. . . . the Lord will be our God and delight to dwell among us, as his own people and will command a blessing upon us in all our ways, so that we shall see much more of his wisdom, power, goodness, and truth than formerly we have been acquainted with.

We shall find that the God of Israel is among us, when ten of us shall be able to resist a thousand of our enemies, when he shall make us a praise and glory, that men shall say of succeeding plantations: the Lord make it like that of New England: for we must consider that we shall be as a City upon a Hill, the eyes of all people are upon us; so that if we shall deal falsely with our God in this work, we have undertaken and so cause him to withdraw his present help from us, we shall be made a story and a byword through the world, we shall open the mouths of enemies to speak evil of the ways of God and all professors for God's sake; we shall shame the faces of many of God's worthy servants, and cause their prayers to be turned into curses upon us until we be consumed out of the good land whither we are going.

We are commanded this day to love the Lord our God and to love one another to walk in his ways and to keep his commandments and his ordinance, and his laws, and the Articles of our Covenant with him that we may live and be multiplied, and that the Lord our God may bless us in the land whither we go to possess it. Therefore let us choose life, that we, and our seed, may live; by obeying his voice and cleaving to him, for he is our life and our prosperity.

PILGRIMS
they brought the faith

It is the will and command of God, that (since the coming of his son the Lord Jesus) a permission of the most paganish . . . or antichristian consciences and worships be granted to all men in all nations or countries; and they are only to be fought against with that sword which is only able to conquer, to wit, the sword of God's spirit, the word of God.

—ROGER WILLIAMS

We shall be as a city upon a hill . . .

—JOHN WINTHROP

God requireth not an uniformity of religion to be enacted or enforced in any civil state; enforced uniformity (sooner or later) is the greatest occasion of civil war, ravishing of conscience, persecution of Christ Jesus in his servants, and of the hypocrisy and destruction of millions of souls. . . . true civility and Christianity may both flourish in a state or kingdom, notwithstanding the permission of diverse and contrary consciences.

—ROGER WILLIAMS

18

Inasmuch as the great Father has given us this year an abundant harvest of Indian corn, wheat, beans, squashes, and garden vegetables, and has made the forests to abound with game and the sea with fish and clams, and inasmuch as he has protected us from the ravages of the savages, has spared us from pestilence and disease, has granted us freedom to worship God according to the dictates of our own conscience; now, I, your magistrate, do proclaim that all ye Pilgrims, with your wives and little ones, do gather at the meeting house, on the hill, between the hours of nine and twelve in the day time, on Thursday, November the twenty-ninth of the year of our Lord one thousand six hundred and twenty-three, and the third year since the Pilgrims landed . . . there to listen to the pastor, and render thanksgiving to the Almighty God for all his blessings.

—WILLIAM BRADFORD

It is admirable to consider the power of faith, by which all things are (almost) possible to be done; it can remove mountains (if need were); it hath stayed the course of the sun, raised the dead, cast out devils, reversed the order of nature, quenched the violence of the fire, made the water become firm footing for Peter to walk on. . . . Faith is not only thus potent, but it is so necessary that without faith there is no salvation; therefore with all our seedings and gettings, let us above all seek to obtain this pearl of price.

—ANNE BRADSTREET

Man, as he stands in relation to man simply hath liberty to do what he lists; it is a liberty to do evil as well as good. This liberty is incompatible and inconsistent with authority. . . . But if you will be satisfied to enjoy such civil and lawful liberties, such as Christ allows you, then will you quietly and cheerfully submit unto that authority which is set over you . . . for your good.

—JOHN WINTHROP

AMERICA THE BEAUTIFUL

KATHARINE LEE BATES

O beautiful for spacious skies,
For amber waves of grain,
For purple mountain majesties
Above the fruited plain!
America! America!
God shed his grace on thee,
And crown thy good with brotherhood
From sea to shining sea!

O beautiful for pilgrim feet,
Whose stern impassioned stress
A thoroughfare for freedom beat
Across the wilderness!
America! America!
God mend thine ev'ry flaw,
Confirm thy soul in self-control,
Thy liberty in law.

O beautiful for heroes proved
In liberating strife,
Who more than self their country loved,
And mercy more than life!
America! America!
May God thy gold refine,
Till all success be nobleness
And every gain divine!

O beautiful for patriot dream
That sees, beyond the years,
Thine alabaster cities gleam
Undimmed by human tears!
America! America!
God shed his grace on thee,
And crown thy good with brotherhood
From sea to shining sea!

Sunrise and tidepool, Gulf Islands National Seashore, Santa
Rosa Island, Florida. © William H. Johnson (51089-00112).

PARADISE IN AMERICA

Jonathan Edwards, 1734

It is not unlikely that this work of God's spirit, that is so extraordinary and wonderful, is the dawning, or at least, a prelude of that glorious work of God, so often foretold in Scripture, which in the progress and issue of it shall renew the world of mankind. If we consider how long since, the things foretold, as what should precede this great event have been accomplished; and how long this event has been expected by the church of God, and thought to be nigh by the most eminent men of God in the church; and withal consider what the state of things now is, and has for a considerable time been, in the church of God, and world of mankind, we cannot reasonably think otherwise, than that the beginning of this great work of God must be near. And there are many things that make it probable that this work will begin in America. . . .

It is agreeable to God's manner of working, when he accomplishes any glorious work in the world, to introduce a new and more excellent state of his church, to begin his work where his church had not been till then, and where was no foundation already laid, that the power of God might be the more conspicuous; that the work might appear to be entirely God's, and be more manifestly a creation out of nothing. . . . When God is about to turn the earth into a Paradise, he does not begin his work where there is some good growth already, but in a wilderness, where nothing grows, and nothing is to be seen but dry sand and barren rocks; that the light may shine out of darkness, and the world be replenished from emptiness, and the earth watered by springs from a droughty desert; agreeably to many prophecies of Scripture. . .

And if we may suppose that this glorious work of God shall begin in any part of America, I think if we consider the circumstances of the settlement of New England, it must needs appear the most likely of all American colonies, to be the place whence this work shall principally take its rise.

And if these things are so, it gives more abundant reason to hope

22

that what is now seen in America, and especially in New England, may prove
the dawn of that glorious day: and the very uncommon and wonderful circumstances and events of this work, seem to me strongly to argue that God
intends it as the beginning or forerunner of something vastly great.

WRITINGS

Fra Junípero Serra

Mission arch covered with beautiful bougainvillea at the Mission of San Juan Capistrano, California. © M. Gibson/H. Armstrong Roberts (KH-12404-g).

The day came. A little chapel and altar were erected in that little valley, and under the same live-oak, close to the beach where it is said Mass was celebrated at the beginning of the last century. Two processions from different directions converged at the same time on the spot, one from the sea, and one from the land expedition; we singing the divine praises in the launch, and the men on land in their hearts.

Our arrival was greeted by the joyful sound of the bells suspended from the branches of the oak tree. Everything being in readiness. . . . I intoned the hymn *"Veni, Reator Spiritus,"* at the conclusion of which, and after invoking the help of the Holy Spirit on everything we were about to perform, I blessed the salt and the water. Then we all made our way to a gigantic cross which was all in readiness and lying on the ground. With everyone lending a hand we set it in an upright position. . . . All the time the bells were ringing, and our rifles were being fired, and from the boat came the thunder of big guns.

24

GOD BLESS AMERICA

IRVING BERLIN

While the storm clouds gather
Far across the sea,
Let us swear allegiance
To a land that's free;
Let us all be grateful
For a land so fair,
As we raise our voices
In a solemn prayer.

God bless America,
Land that I love,
Stand beside her and guide her
Through the night with a light from above.
From the mountains, to the prairies,
To the oceans white with foam,
God bless America
My home sweet home
God bless America
My home sweet home.

Martin's House Inn, Nantucket Island, Massachusetts.
© William H. Johnson (22293-01011).

THE SPIRIT OF LIBERTY

WASHINGTON CROSSING THE DELAWARE RIVER by Emanuel
Gottlieb Leutze. Metropolitan Museum of Art, New York,
New York. © SuperStock (262-1726).

W here, say some, is the king of America? I'll tell you, friend, he reigns above, and doth not make havoc of mankind like the Royal Brute of Great Britain. Yet that may not appear to be defective even in earthly honors, let a day be solemnly set apart for proclaiming the charter; let it be brought forth placed upon the divine law, the Word of God; let a crown be placed thereon, by which the world may know, that so far as we approve of monarchy, that in America THE LAW IS KING.

For as in absolute governments the king is law, so in free countries the law ought to be king, and there ought to be no other. But lest any ill use should afterwards arise, let the crown at the conclusion of the ceremony be demolished, and scattered among the people whose right it is. . . .

O ye that love mankind! Ye that dare oppose not only the tyranny but the tyrant, stand forth! Every spot of the old world is overrun with oppression. Freedom hath been hunted round the globe. Asia and Africa have long expelled her. Europe regards her like a stranger, and England hath given her warning to depart. O receive the fugitive, and prepare in time an asylum for mankind.

FROM COMMON SENSE

Thomas Paine, 1776

United States Supreme Court, Washington, D.C. © Neal Slavin/SuperStock (450H-175).

30

SPEECH TO THE SECOND VIRGINIA CONVENTION

Patrick Henry, 1775

I ask gentlemen, sir, what means this martial array, if its purpose be not to force us to submission? Can gentlemen assign any other possible motives for it? Has Great Britain any enemy, in this quarter of the world, to call for all this accumulation of navies and armies? No, sir, she has none. They are meant for us; they can be meant for no other. They are sent over to bind and rivet upon us those chains which the British ministry have been so long forging. And what have we to oppose to them?

Shall we try argument? Sir, we have been trying that for the last ten years. Have we anything new to offer on the subject? Nothing. We have held the subject up in every light of which it is capable; but it has been all in vain. Shall we resort to entreaty and humble supplication? What terms shall we find which have not been already exhausted? Let us not, I beseech you, sir, deceive ourselves longer. Sir, we have done everything that could be done to avert the storm which is now coming on. We have petitioned; we have remonstrated; we have supplicated; we have prostrated ourselves before the tyrannical hands of the ministry and parliament. Our petitions have been slighted; our remonstrances have produced additional violence and insult; our supplications have been disregarded; and we have been spurned, with contempt, from the foot of the throne. In vain, after these things, may we indulge the fond hope of peace and reconciliation. There is no longer any room for hope. If we wish to be free—if we mean to preserve inviolate those inestimable privileges for which we have been so long contending—if we mean not basely to abandon the noble struggle in which we have been so long engaged and which we have pledged ourselves never to abandon until the glorious object of our contest shall be obtained, we must fight! I repeat it, sir, we must fight! An appeal to arms and to the God of Hosts is all that is left us!

They tell us, sir, that we are weak; unable to cope with so formidable an adversary. But when shall we be stronger? Will it be the next week, or the next year? Will it be when we are totally disarmed, and when a British guard shall be stationed in every house? Shall we gather strength by irresolution and inaction? Shall we acquire the means of effectual resistance by lying supinely on our backs, and hugging the delusive phantom of hope, until our enemies shall have bound us hand and foot? Sir, we are not weak, if we make a proper use of the means which the God of nature hath placed in our power. Three millions of people, armed in the holy cause of liberty, and in such a country as that which we possess, are invincible by any force which our enemy can send against us. Besides, sir, we shall not fight our battles alone.

There is a just God who presides over the destinies of nations; and who will raise friends to fight our battles for us. The battle, sir, is not to the strong alone; it is to the vigilant, the active, the brave. Besides, sir, we have no election. If we were base enough to desire it, it is now too late to retire from the contest. There is no retreat but in submission and slavery! Our chains are forged! Their clanking may be heard on the plains of Boston! The war is inevitable—and let it come! I repeat it, sir, let it come!

It is vain, sir, to extenuate the matter. Gentlemen may cry peace, peace—but there is no peace. The war is actually begun! The next gale that sweeps from the North will bring to our ears the clash of resounding arms! Our brethren are already in the field! Why stand we here idle? What is it that gentlemen wish? What would they have? Is life so dear, or peace so sweet, as to be purchased at the price of chains and slavery? Forbid it, Almighty God! I know not what course others may take; but as for me, give me liberty, or give me death!

DECLARATION OF INDEPENDENCE OF THE UNITED STATES OF AMERICA

1776

Independence Hall, Philadelphia, Pennsylvania. © Gala/SuperStock (191-191C).

W hen in the Course of human events, it becomes necessary for one people to dissolve the political bands which have connected them with another, and to assume among the powers of the earth, the separate and equal station to which the Laws of Nature and of Nature's God entitle them, a decent respect to the opinions of mankind requires that they should declare the causes which impel them to the separation.

We hold these truths to be self-evident, that all men are created equal, that they are endowed by their Creator with certain unalienable Rights, that among these are Life, Liberty, and the pursuit of Happiness— That to secure these rights, Governments are instituted among Men, deriving their just Powers from the consent of the governed, that whenever any Form of Government becomes destructive of these ends, it is the Right of the People to alter or to abolish it, and to institute new Government, laying its foundation on such principles and organizing its powers in such form, as to them shall seem most likely to effect their Safety and Happiness. . . .

34

THE SPIRIT OF LIBERTY

THE LIBERTY BELL

AUTHOR UNKNOWN

There was tumult in the city in the quaint old Quaker town,
And the streets were rife with people, pacing restless up and down,
People gathering at corners where they whispered, each to each,
And the sweat stood on their temples, with the earnestness of speech.

As the bleak Atlantic currents lash the wild Newfoundland shore,
So they beat against the State House, so they surged against the door;
And the mingling of their voices made a harmony profound,
Till the quiet street of Chestnut was all turbulent with sound.

"Will they do it?"—"Dare they do it?" "Who is speaking?"—"What's the news?"
"What of Adams?" "What of Sherman?" "Oh, God grant they won't refuse!"
Aloft in that high steeple sat the bellman, old and gray;
He was weary of the tyrant and his iron-sceptered sway;
So he sat with one hand ready on the clapper of the bell,
When his eye should catch the signal, very happy news to tell.

See! See! the dense crowd quivers through all its lengthy line,
As the boy beside the portal looks forth to give the sign.
With his small hands upward lifted, breezes dallying with his hair,
Hark! with deep, clear intonation, breaks his young voice on the air.

Hushed the people's swelling murmur, list the boy's strong, joyous cry,
"Ring!" he shouts alone, "Ring, Grandpa! Ring! Oh, ring for Liberty!"
And, straightway, at the signal, the old bellman lifts his hand,
And sends the good news, making iron music through the land.

How they shouted! What rejoicing! How the old bell shook the air,
Till the clang of Freedom ruffled the calm, gliding Delaware!
How the bonfires and the torches illumed the night's repose!
And from the flames, like Phoenix, fair Liberty arose!

That old bell now is silent, and hushed its iron tongue,
But the spirit it awakened still lives—forever young.
And, while we greet the sunlight, on the fourth of each July,
We'll ne'er forget the bellman who, 'twixt the earth and sky,
Rung out *Our Independence;* which, please God, shall never die!

AUTOBIOGRAPHY

Benjamin Franklin, 1771

BENJAMIN FRANKLIN by David Martin, from the collection of the White House Historical Association. © Stock Montage/SuperStock (1047-260).

And now I speak of thanking God, I desire with all Humility to acknowledge, that I owe the mention'd Happiness of my past Life to his kind Providence, which led me to the Means I us'd and gave them Success. . . .

I had been religiously educated as a Presbyterian; and tho' some of the dogmas of that persuasion, such as the eternal decrees of God, election, reprobation, etc., appeared to me unintelligible, others doubtful, and I early absented myself from the public assemblies of the sect, Sunday being my studying day, I never was without some religious principles. I never doubted, for instance, the existence of the Deity; that he made the world, and govern'd it by his Providence; that the most acceptable service of God was the doing good to man; that our souls are immortal; and that all crime will be punished, and virtue rewarded, either here or hereafter. These I esteem'd the essentials of every religion; and, being to be found in all the religions we had in our country, I respected them all, tho' with different degrees of respect, as I found them more or less mix'd with other articles, which, without any tendency to inspire, promote, or conform morality, serv'd principally to divide us, and make us unfriendly to one another. This respect to all, with an opinion that the worst had some good effect, induc'd me to avoid all discourse that might tend to lessen the good opinion another might have of his own religion; and as our province increas'd in people, and new places of worship were continually wanted, and generally erected by voluntary contribution, my mite for such purpose, whatever might be the sect, was never refused. . . .

Here is my creed. I believe in one God, the Creator of the universe. That he governs it by his providence. That he ought to be worshiped. That the most acceptable service we render to him is doing good to his other children. That the soul of man is immortal, and will be treated with justice in another life respecting its conduct in this.

AMERICA
SAMUEL FRANCIS SMITH

My country 'tis of thee
Sweet land of liberty;
Of thee I sing.
Land where my fathers died
Land of the pilgrims' pride
From every mountainside
        Let freedom ring.

My native country—thee
Land of the noble free,
        Thy name I love;
I love thy rocks and rills
Thy woods and templed hills
My heart with rapture thrills
        Like that above.

Let music swell the breeze
And ring from all the trees
        Sweet freedom's song
Let all that breathe partake
Let mortal tongues awake
Let rocks their silence break
        The sound prolong.

Our fathers' God, to thee
Author of liberty
        To thee we sing.
Long may our land be bright
With freedom's holy light;
Protect us by thy might,
        Great God, our King.

A flag flutters in the breeze as it hangs from the front porch.
© Bluestone Procductions/SuperStock (1292R-800).

41

THE BIRTH OF A NATION

John Adams, JULY 3, 1776

THE DECLARATION OF
INDEPENDENCE, by
John Trumbull. © H.
Armstrong Roberts
KH-10843-J).

Yesterday, the greatest question was decided which ever was debated in America, and a greater, perhaps, never was nor will be decided among men. A resolution was passed without one dissenting colony, "that these united colonies are, and of right ought to be, free and independent states, and as such they have, and of right ought to have, full power to make war, conclude peace, establish commerce, and to do all other acts and things which other states may rightfully do."

You will see in a few days a declaration setting forth the causes which have impelled us to this mighty revolution, and the reasons which will justify it in the sight of God and man. A plan of confederation will be taken up in a few days.

You will think me transported with enthusiasm, but I am not. I am well aware of the toil, and blood, and treasure that it will cost us to maintain this declaration, and support and defend these states. Yet, through all the gloom, I can see the rays of ravishing light and glory. I can see that the end is more than worth all the means, and that posterity will triumph in that day's transaction, even although we should rue it, which I trust in God we shall not.

42

43

THE SPIRIT OF LIBERTY

INDEPENDENCE

they kept the faith

It is essential to turn back to our history now and then to remind ourselves of the principles on which this nation is based. . . . We could never have conquered the wilderness; never have built the foundations of a country and a new concept of life, based on the fullest and freest development of the individual; never have overcome vast difficultics and dangcrs; if wc had not had a new idea, an idea so noble in concept that it gave us confidence in ourselves and gave us the strength to build this new nation, step by step.

—Eleanor Roosevelt

As for me, give me liberty, or give me death!

—Patrick Henry

Here is my creed. I believe in one God, the Creator of the universe. That he governs it by his providence. That he ought to be worshiped. That the most acceptable service we render to him is doing good to his other children. That the soul of man is immortal and will be treated with justice in another life respecting its conduct in this.

—Benjamin Franklin

44

The second day of July 1776 will be the most memorable epoch in the history of America. I am apt to believe that it will be celebrated by succeeding generations as the great anniversary festival. It ought to be commemorated as the day of deliverance, by solemn acts of devotion to God Almighty. It ought to be solemnized with pomp and parade, with shows, games, sports, guns, bells, bonfires, and illuminations, from one end of this continent to the other, from this time forward for evermore.

—John Adams

I long to hear that you have declared an independency—and by the way, in the new Code of Laws which I suppose it will be necessary for you to make, I desire you would remember the ladies, and be more generous and favorable to them than your ancestors. Do not put such unlimited power into the hands of the husbands. Remember all men would be tyrants if they could. If particular care and attention is not paid to the ladies we are determined to foment a rebellion, and will not hold ourselves bound by any laws in which we have no voice or representation.

—Abigail Adams

The God who gave us life gave us liberty at the same time.

—Thomas Jefferson

Let us compare every constitution we have seen with that of the United States of America, and we shall have no reason to blush for our country. On the contrary, we shall feel the strongest motives to fall upon our knees, in gratitude to heaven for having graciously pleased to give us birth and education in that country, and for having destined us to live under her laws!

—John Adams

FOURTH OF JULY

BETTY W. STOFFEL

Let there be prayers as well as great parades.
Let hymns combine with patriotic songs.
Let there be leaders of the future days
With heroes of the past amid the throngs.
Let reverent silence punctuate the noise.
Let God be praised for this great land of ours.
Let sober meditation balance joys
And grave humility mark crucial hours.

Let statesmanship grow from this nation's need.
Let citizenship be equal to these days,
That godly men who gave their lives indeed
Be not betrayed by dull, indifferent ways.
Let joyfulness, not wildness, mark the free,
That God may find us worth our liberty!

FIRST INAUGURAL ADDRESS

George Washington

APRIL 30, 1789

Statue of George Washington in prayer, Freedom Foundation, Valley Forge, Pennsylvania. © H. Armstrong Roberts (KH-3600).

48

Among the vicissitudes incident to life, no event could have filled me with greater anxieties than that of which the notification was transmitted by your order and received on the fourteenth day of the present month.

On the one hand, I was summoned by my country, whose voice I can never hear but with veneration and love. . . . On the other hand, the magnitude and difficulty of the trust to which the voice of my country called me . . . could not but overwhelm with despondence one who . . . ought to be peculiarly conscious of his own deficiencies. . . .

It would be peculiarly improper to omit, in this first official act, my fervent supplications to that Almighty Being who rules over the universe, who presides in the councils of nations, and whose providential aids can supply every human defect, that His benediction may consecrate to the liberties and happiness of the people of the United States, a government instituted by themselves for these essential purposes, and may enable every instrument employed in its administration to execute with success the functions allotted to his charge.

In tendering this homage to the Great Author of every public and private good, I assure myself that it expresses your sentiments not less than my own, nor those of my fellow citizens at large, less than either. No people can be bound to acknowledge and adore the Invisible Hand which conducts the affairs of men more than the people of the United States. Every step by which they have advanced to the character of an independent nation seems to have been distinguished by some token of providential agency. And in the important revolution just accomplished in the system of their united government, the tranquil deliberations and voluntary consent of so many distinct communities, from which the event has resulted, cannot be compared with the means by which most governments have been established, without some return of pious gratitude, along with a humble anticipation of the future blessings which the past seem to presage. . . .

SAIL ON, O SHIP OF STATE!

HENRY WADSWORTH LONGFELLOW

Thou, too, sail on, O ship of State!
Sail on, O Union, strong and great!
Humanity with all its fears,
With all its hopes of future years,
Is hanging breathless on thy fate!
We know what Master laid thy keel,
What Workmen wrought thy ribs of steel,
Who made each mast, and sail, and rope,
What anvils rang, what hammers beat,
In what a forge and what a heat
Were shaped the anchors of thy hope!

50

United States Capitol, Washington, D.C. © Murat
Ayranci/SuperStock (1131-101).

Fear not each sudden sound and shock,
'Tis of the wave and not the rock;
'Tis but the flapping of the sail,
And not a rent made by the gale!
In spite of rock and tempest's roar,
In spite of false lights on the shore,
Sail on, nor fear to breast the sea!
Our hearts, our hopes, are all with thee,
Our hearts, our hopes, our prayers, our tears,
Our faith, triumphant o'er our fears,
Are all with thee—are all with thee!

51

W e the People of the United States, in order to form a more perfect Union, establish justice, insure domestic tranquility, provide for the common defence, promote the general welfare, and secure the Blessings of liberty to ourselves and our posterity, do ordain and establish this Constitution for the United States of America. . . .

FROM THE CONSTITUTION OF THE UNITED STATES OF AMERICA

1789

Bill of Rights

Article 1. Congress shall make no law respecting an establishment of religion, or prohibiting the free exercise thereof; or abridging the freedom of speech, or of the press; or the right of the people peaceably to assemble, and to petition the Government for a redress of grievances.

Article 2. A well-regulated militia, being necessary to the security of a free State, the right of the people to keep and bear Arms, shall not be infringed.

Article 3. No soldier shall, in time of peace be quartered in any house, without the consent of the owner, nor in time of war, but in a manner to be prescribed by law.

Article 4. The right of the people to be secure in their persons, houses, papers, and effects, against unreasonable searches and seizures, shall not be violated, and no warrants shall issue, but upon probable cause, supported by oath or affirmation, and particularly describing the place to be searched, and the persons or things to be seized.

Article 5. No person shall be held to answer for a capital, or otherwise infamous crime, unless on a presentment or indictment of a Grand Jury, except in cases arising in the land or naval forces, or in the militia, when in actual service in time of war or public danger; nor shall any person be subject for the same offense to be twice put in jeopardy of life or limb; nor shall be compelled in any criminal case to be a witness against himself, nor be deprived of life, liberty, or property, without due process of law; nor shall private property be taken for public use, without just compensation.

Article 6. In all criminal prosecutions, the accused shall enjoy the right of a speedy and public trial, by an impartial jury of the State and district wherein the crime shall have been committed, which district shall have been previously ascertained

Detail of the United States Constitution. © S. Feld/H. Armstrong Roberts (KH-12308).

52

by law, and to be informed of the nature and cause of the accusation; to be confronted with the witnesses against him; to have compulsory process for obtaining witnesses in his favor; and to have the assistance of counsel for his defense.

Article 7. In suits at common law, where the value in controversy shall exceed twenty dollars, the right of trial by jury shall be preserved, and no fact tried by jury shall be otherwise re-examined in any court of the United States, than according to the rules of the common law.

Article 8. Excessive bail shall not be required, nor excessive fines imposed, nor cruel and unusual punishments inflicted.

Article 9. The enumeration in the Constitution of certain rights shall not be construed to deny or disparage others retained by the people.

Article 10. The powers not delegated to the United States by the Constitution, nor prohibited by it to the States, are reserved to the States respectively, or to the people.

A NATIONAL PRAYER

Thomas Jefferson

The Jefferson
Memorial, Washington,
D.C. © Yoshio
Tomii/SuperStock
(1269-483).

Almighty God, who has given us this good land for our heritage, we humbly beseech thee that we may always prove ourselves a people mindful of thy favor and glad to do thy will.

Bless our land with honorable industry, sound learning, and pure manners. Save us from violence, discord and confusion, from pride and arrogance, and from every evil way. Defend our liberties, and fashion into one united people the multitude brought hither out of many kindreds and tongues.

Endow with the spirit of wisdom those to whom in thy name we entrust the authority of government, that there may be justice and peace at home, and that through obedience to thy law, we may show forth thy praise among the nations of the earth.

In time of prosperity, fill our hearts with thankfulness, and, in the day of trouble, suffer not our trust in thee to fail; all of which we ask through Jesus Christ our Lord. Amen.

FAREWELL ADDRESS

George Washington

SEPTEMBER 17, 1796

Mount Vernon,
Virginia, home of
George Washington.
© Scott Barrow,
Inc./SuperStock (59-
2327B).

The unity of government which constitutes you one people is also now dear to you. It is justly so, for it is a main pillar in the edifice of your real independence, the support of your tranquility at home, your peace abroad, of your safety, of your prosperity, of that very liberty which you so highly prize. . . .

The name of American, which belongs to you in your national capacity, must always exalt the just pride of patriotism more than any appellation derived from local discriminations. With slight shades of difference, you have the same religion, manners, habits, and political principles. You have in a common cause fought and triumphed together. The independence and liberty you possess are the work of joint councils and joint efforts, of common dangers, sufferings, and successes. . . .

Of all the dispositions and habits which lead to political prosperity, religion and morality are indispensable supports. In vain would that man claim the tribute of patriotism who should labor to subvert these great pillars of human happiness, these firmest props of the duties of men and citizens. The mere politician, equally with the pious man, ought to respect and to cherish them. A volume could not trace all their connections with private and public felicity. Let it simply be asked: Where is the security for property, for reputation, for life, if the sense of religious obligation desert the oaths which are the instruments of investigation in courts of justice? And let us with caution indulge the supposition that morality can be maintained without religion. Whatever may be conceded to the influence of refined education on minds of peculiar structure, reason and experience both forbid us to expect that national morality can prevail in exclusion of religious principle. . . .

56

THE SPIRIT OF LIBERTY

THE STAR-SPANGLED BANNER

FRANCIS SCOTT KEY

Oh say, can you see, by the dawn's early light,
What so proudly we hailed at the twilight's last gleaming,
Whose broad stripes and bright stars through the perilous fight,
O'er the ramparts we watched were so gallantly streaming?
And the rockets' red glare, the bombs bursting in air,
Gave proof thro' the night that our flag was still there.
Oh, say, does that star-spangled banner yet wave
O'er the land of the free and the home of the brave!

On the shore, dimly seen thro' the mists of the deep,
Where the foe's haughty host in dread silence reposes,
What is that which the breeze, o'er the towering steep,
As it fitfully blows, half conceals, half discloses?
Now it catches the gleam of the morning's first beam,
In full glory reflected, now shines in the stream.
'Tis the star-spangled banner; oh, long may it wave
O'er the land of the free, and the home of the brave!

And where is that band who so vauntingly swore
That the havoc of war and the battle's confusion
A home and a country should leave us no more?
Their blood has washed out their foul footsteps' pollution.
No refuge could save the hireling and slave
From the terror of flight or the gloom of the grave:
And the star-spangled banner in triumph doth wave
O'er the land of the free and the home of the brave!

Oh, thus be it ever, when freemen shall stand
Between their loved homes and the war's desolation;
Blest with victory and peace, may the heaven-rescued land
Praise the power that hath made and preserved us a nation!
Then conquer we must, when our cause it is just,
And this be our motto: "In God is our trust!"
And the star-spangled banner in triumph shall wave,
O'er the land of the free, and the home of the brave!

Flags wave along a street in Staten Island, New York, New
York. © Anthony Butera/SuperStock (2026-259).

59

THE AMERICAN IDEA

Theodore H. White, 1986

Overlooking the lush farmland in Columbia County, Wisconsin. © by Darryl R. Beers (MT-70J69-91).

The idea was there at the very beginning, well before Thomas Jefferson put it into words—and the idea rang the call. Jefferson himself could not have imagined the reach of his call across the world in time to come when he wrote: "We hold these truths to be self-evident, that all men are created equal, that they are endowed by their Creator with certain unalienable rights, that among these are life, liberty and the pursuit of happiness."

But over the next two centuries the call would reach the potato patches of Ireland, the ghettoes of Europe, the paddyfields of China, stirring farmers to leave their lands and townsmen their trades and thus unsettling all traditional civilizations. It is the call from Thomas Jefferson, embodied in the great statue that looks down the Narrows of New York Harbor, and in the immigrants who answered the call, that we now celebrate.

Some of the first European Americans had come to the new continent to worship God in their own way, others to seek their fortunes. But over a century-and-a-half, the new world changed those Europeans, above all the Englishmen who had come to North America. Neither king nor court nor church could stretch over the ocean to the wild continent. To survive, the first emigrants had to learn to govern themselves. But the freedom of the wilderness whetted their appetites for more freedoms. By the time Jefferson drafted his call, men were in the field fighting for those new-learned freedoms, killing and being killed by English soldiers, the best-trained troops in the world, supplied by the world's greatest navy. Only something worth dying for could unite American volunteers and keep them in the field—a stated cause, a flag, a nation they could call their own.

When on the Fourth of July 1776, the colonial leaders who had been meeting as a Continental Congress in Philadelphia voted to approve Jefferson's Declaration of Independence, it was not puffed-up rhetoric for them to pledge to each other "our lives, our fortunes and our sacred honor."

Unless their new "United States of America" won the war, the Congressmen would be judged traitors as relentlessly as would the irregulars-under-arms in the field. . . .

The new Americans were tough men fighting for a very tough idea. How they won their battle is a story for the schoolbooks, studied by scholars, wrapped in myths by historians and poets. But what is most important is the story of the idea that made them into a nation, the idea that had an explosive power undreamed of in 1776. All other nations had come into being among people whose families had lived for time out of mind on the same land where they were born. . . . But Americans are a nation born of an idea; not the place, but the idea created the United States Government.

61

The Underground Railway by Charles T. Webber.
© SuperStock (900-128791).

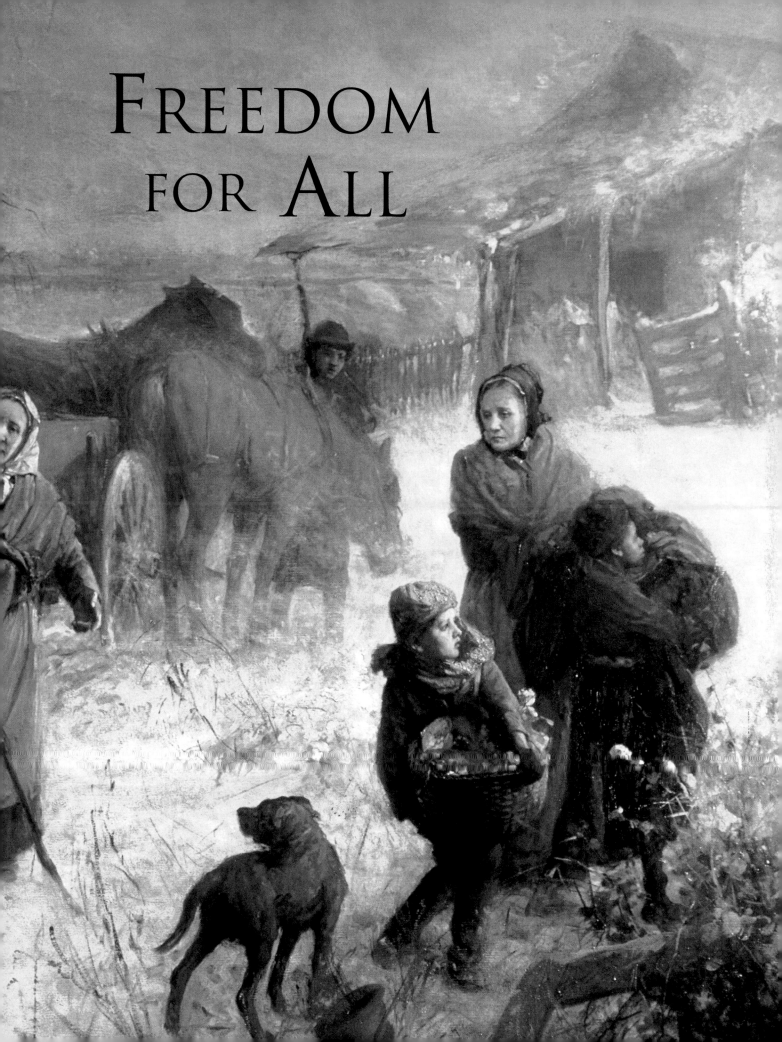

FREEDOM
FOR ALL

CHIEF SEATTLE'S ORATION

Chief Seattle, 1854

Bust of Chief Seattle Sculpture/Relief. © SuperStock (2675-583682).

A few more moons. A few more winters—and not one of the descendants of the mighty hosts that once moved over this broad land or lived in happy homes, protected by the Great Spirit, will remain to mourn over the graves of a people—once more powerful and hopeful than yours. But why should I mourn at the untimely fate of my people? Tribe follows tribe, and nation follows nation, like the waves of the sea. It is the order of nature, and regret is useless. Your time of decay may be distant, but it will surely come, for even the White Man whose God walked and talked with him as friend with friend, cannot be exempt from the common destiny. We may be brothers after all. We will see.

We will ponder your proposition and when we decide we will let you know. But should we accept it, I here and now make this condition that we will not be denied the privilege without molestation of visiting at any time the tombs of our ancestors, friends and children. Every part of this soil is sacred in the estimation of my people. Every hillside, every valley, every plain and grove, has been hallowed by some sad or happy event in days long vanished. Even the rocks, which seem to be dumb and dead as they swelter in the sun along the silent shore, thrill with memories of stirring events connected with the lives of my people, and the very dust upon which you now stand responds more lovingly to their footsteps than to yours, because it is rich with the blood of our ancestors and our bare feet are conscious of the sympathetic touch. Our departed braves, fond mothers, glad, happy-hearted maidens, and even the little children who lived here and rejoiced here for brief season, will love these somber solitudes and at eventide they greet shadowy returning spirits. And when the last Red Man shall have perished, and the memory of my tribe shall have become a myth among the White Men, these shores will swarm with the invisible dead of my tribe, and when your children's children think themselves alone in the field, the store, the shop, upon the highways, or in the silence of the pathless woods, they will not be alone. In all the earth there is no place dedicated to solitude. At night when the streets of your cities and villages are silent and you think them deserted, they will throng with the returning hosts that once filled them and still love this beautiful land.

Let him be just and deal kindly with my people, for the dead are not powerless. Dead, did I say? There is no death, only a change of worlds.

APPEAL TO THE ROYAL GOVERNOR OF MASSACHUSETTS

1774

Old State House, Boston, Massachusetts. © Witold Skrypczak/SuperStock (1299-804).

The Petition of a Grate Number of Blacks of this Province who by divine permission are held in a state of Slavery within the bowels of a free and Christian Country

Humbly Shewing

That your Petitioners apprehend we have in common with all other men a nature right to our freedoms without Being depriv'd of them by our fellow men as we are a freeborn Pepel and have never forfeited this Blessing by any compact or agreement whatever. But we were unjustly dragged by the cruel hand of power from our dearest friends and sum of us stolen from the bosoms of our tender Parents and from a Populous Pleasant and plentiful country and Brought hither to be made slaves for Life in a Christian land.

Thus we are deprived of every thing that hath a tendency to make life even tolerable, the endearing ties of husband and wife we are strangers to for we are no longer man and wife than our masteres or mistresses thinkes proper marred or onmarred. Our children are also taken from us by force and sent maney miles from us wear we seldom or ever see them again there to be made slaves of for Life which sumtimes is vere short by Reson of Being dragged from their mothers Breest Thus our Lives are imbittered to us on these accounts By our deplorable situation we are rendered incapable of shewing our obedience to Almighty God how can a slave perform the duties of a husband to a wife or parent to his child How can a husband leave master to work and cleave to his wife How can the wife submit themselves to there husbands in all things How can the child obey their parents in all things. There is a great number of us sencear . . . members of the Church of Christ how can the master and the slave be said to fulfill that command Live in love let Brotherly Love contuner and abound Beare yea one another's Bordenes How can the master be said to Beare my Borden when he Beares me down with the Have chanes of slavery and operson against my will and

how can we fulfill our parte of duty to him whilst in this condition and as we cannot serve our God as we ought whilst in this situation. . . .

We therefor Bage your Excellency and Honours will give this its deer weight and consideration and that you will accordingly cause an act of the legislative to be passed that we may obtain our Natural right our freedoms and our children be set at lebety at the years of twenty one for whoues sekes more petequeley your Petitioners is in Duty ever to pray.

67

LIFT EV'RY VOICE AND SING

JAMES WELDON JOHNSON AND J. ROSAMOND JOHNSON, 1900

Left ev'ry voice and sing,
Till earth and heaven ring,
Ring with the harmonies of Liberty;
Let our rejoicing rise
High as the list'ning skies,
Let it resound loud as the rolling sea.
Sing a song full of the faith that the dark past has taught us
Sing a song full of the hope that the present has brought us
Facing the rising sun of our new day begun,
Let us march on till victory is won.

Stony the road we trod,
Bitter the chast'ning rod,
Felt in the days when hope unborn had died;
Yet with a steady beat,
Have not our weary feet
Come to the place for which our fathers sighed?
We have come over a way that with tears has been watered
We have come, treading our path thro' the blood of the slaughtered,
Out from the gloomy past, till now we stand at last
Where the white gleam of our bright star is cast.

God of our weary years,
God of our silent tears,
Thou who hast brought us thus far on the way;
Thou who hast by Thy might,
Led us into the light,
Keep us forever in the path, we pray.

Lest our feet stray from the places, our God, where we met Thee,
Lest our hearts, drunk with the wine of the world, we forget Thee;
Shadowed beneath Thy hand, may we forever stand,
True to our God, true to our native land.

SOUTHERN PLANTATION by William Aiken Walker, 1838-1921.
© David David Gallery/SuperStock (849-10033).

FREEDOM FOR ALL

INDEPENDENCE DAY SPEECH

Frederick Douglass, 1852

Fellow citizens, pardon me, allow me to ask, why am I called upon to speak here today? What have I, or those I represent, to do with your national independence? . . . The blessings in which you, this day, rejoice are not enjoyed in common. The rich inheritance of justice, liberty, prosperity, and independence bequeathed by your fathers is shared by you, not by me. The sunlight that brought light and healing to you has brought stripes and death to me. This Fourth of July is yours, not mine. You may rejoice, I must mourn. To drag a man in fetters into the grand illuminated temple of liberty, and call upon him to join you in joyous anthems, were inhuman mockery and sacrilegious irony. . . .

Fellow citizens, above your national, tumultuous joy, I hear the mournful wail of millions whose chains, heavy and grievous yesterday, are, today, rendered more intolerable by the jubilee shouts that reach them. . . . I do not hesitate to declare with all my soul that the character and conduct of this nation never looked blacker to me than on this Fourth of July. Whether we turn to the declarations of the past or to the professions of the present, the conduct of the nation seems equally hideous and revolting. America is false to the past, false to the present, and solemnly binds herself to be false to the future. Standing with God and the crushed and bleeding slave on this occasion, I will, in the name of humanity which is outraged, in the name of liberty which is fettered, in the name of the Constitution and the Bible which are disregarded and trampled upon, dare to call in question and to denounce, with all the emphasis I can command, everything that serves to perpetuate slavery—the great sin and shame of America! . . .

It is not light that is needed, but fire; it is not the gentle shower, but thunder. We need the storm, the whirlwind, and the earthquake. The feeling of the nation must be quickened; the conscience of the nation must be roused; the propriety of the nation must be startled; the hypocrisy of the nation must be exposed; and its crimes against God and man must be proclaimed and denounced.

A field of purple lupines grow in Carmel Valley, California. © Carr Clifton.

70

ANTISLAVERY CONVENTION ADDRESS

Angelina Grimké, 1838

D o you ask, "What has the North to do with slavery?" Hear it, hear it! Those voices without tell us that the spirit of slavery is here and has been roused to wrath by our conventions; for surely liberty would not foam and tear herself with rage, because her friends are multiplied daily, and meetings are held in quick succession to set forth her virtues and extend her peaceful kingdom. This opposition shows that slavery has done its deadliest work in the hearts of our citizens. . . .

As a Southerner, I feel that it is my duty to stand up here tonight and bear testimony against slavery. I have seen it! I have seen it! I know it has horrors that can never be described. I was brought up under its wing. I witnessed for many years its demoralizing influences and its destructiveness to human happiness. I have never seen a happy slave. I have seen him dance in his chains, but he was not happy. There is a wide difference between happiness and mirth. Man cannot enjoy happiness while his manhood is destroyed. Slaves, however, may be, and sometimes are mirthful. When hope is extinguished, they say, "Let us eat and drink, for tomorrow we die." . . .

I thank the Lord that there is yet life enough left to feel the truth, even though it rages at it; that conscience is not so completely seared as to be unmoved by the truth of the living God. . . .

THE OLD COTTON PICKER BY William Aiken Walker, 1838-1921. © Christie's Images/SuperStock (1100-589).

73

Letter from a Union Soldier

George W. Harvey

April 10, 1864

Dear Ana, it is again Sunday and we have gone through with our weekly inspection. I know of no way in which I can spend my time so agreeably as in writing to loved ones at homes. . . . We have had one of the most torrential rains since yesterday morning since I have been in Virginia. It has stopped raining this morning, sun shines out part of the time; but I think the wet weather is not yet over. There will be no moving of the army until we have some dry weather to dry up the mud. . . . You must keep of good courage, Ana. I know that it requires a good deal of fortitude to sustain one in your place. I deeply sympathize with you. I know your anxiety as on one hand you see your parents about to depart for the spiritland, and on the other, a husband and two sons in the army exposed to the horrors of war. I cannot, I would not, say to you do not feel bad, for it is contrary to your true and undying love to your dear husband and your maternal love for your children not to feel bad in a time like this; but I will say try and keep up as good courage as you can. Do not look on the dark side alone. Remember the darkest time is just before day.

We must put our trust in our heavenly Father, hoping that the day star of peace will soon dawn on our land and that we shall all meet again. . . . When I see those slave mothers fleeing from bondage with their little children pressed to their bosoms and see little children with scarcely clothing enough to cover their nakedness, weary with their long marches by night through the roads and see the joy that lights up their countenances when they feel that they are safe within our lines, that they are free, that their children are not to be torn from their fond embrace, I feel that we are engaged in a holy cause, one that God will bless and prosper. I will write to you again in a few days. Your affectionate husband, . . .

Slave Market by Eyre Crowe, 1824-1910. © SuperStock (2180-486291).

74

EMANCIPATION PROCLAMATION

Abraham Lincoln, 1862

Emancipation Proclamation, 1862. © SuperStock (900-139800).

Whereas on the 22d day of September, A.D. 1862, a proclamation was issued by the President of the United States, containing, among other things, the following, to wit:

That on the 1st day of January, A.D. 1863, all persons held as slaves within any State or designated part of a State the people whereof shall then be in rebellion against the United States shall be then, thenceforward, and forever free; and the executive government of the United States, including the military and naval authority thereof, will recognize and maintain the freedom of such persons and will do no act or acts to repress such persons, or any of them, in any efforts they may make for their actual freedom. . . .

Now, therefore, I, Abraham Lincoln, President of the United States, by virtue of the Power in me vested as Commander in Chief of the Army and Navy of the United States in time of actual armed rebellion against the authority and government of the United States, and as a fit and necessary war measure for suppressing said rebellion, do, on this 1st day of January, A.D. 1863, and in accordance with my purpose so to do, publicly proclaimed for the full period of one hundred days from the first day above mentioned, order and designate as the States and parts of States wherein the people thereof, respectively, are this day in rebellion against the United States the following, to wit: . . .

And by virtue of the power and for the purpose aforesaid, I do order and declare that all persons held as slaves within said designated States and parts of States are, and henceforward shall be, free; and that the Executive Government of the United States, including the military and naval authorities thereof, will recognize and maintain the freedom of said persons. . . .

And upon this act, sincerely believed to be an act of justice, warranted by the Constitution upon military necessity, I invoke the considerate judgment of mankind and the gracious favor of Almighty God.

EMANCIPATION PROCLAMATION.

WHEREAS, On the 22nd day of September, A.D. 1862, a proclamation was issued by the President of the UNITED STATES, containing, among other things, the following, to wit:

"That on the 1st day of January, in the year of our Lord one thousand eight hundred and sixty three, all persons held as slaves within any State, or designated part of a State, the people whereof shall then be in rebellion against the UNITED STATES, shall be henceforth and forever FREE; and the Executive Government of the United States, including the Military and Naval authorities thereof, will recognize and maintain the freedom of such persons, and will do no act or acts to repress such persons, or any of them in any effort they may make for their actual freedom; that the Executive will, on the first day of January aforesaid, issue a proclamation designating the States and parts of States, if any, in which the people therein, respectively, shall then be in rebellion against the United States; and the fact that any State, or the people thereof, shall on that day be, in good faith, represented in the Congress of the United States by members chosen thereto, at elections wherein a majority of the qualified voters of such States shall have participated, shall, in the absence of strong countervailing testimony, be deemed conclusive evidence that such State and the people thereof, are not in rebellion against the United States."

Now, THEREFORE, I, ABRAHAM LINCOLN, PRESIDENT of the UNITED STATES, by virtue of the power in me vested as Commander-in-Chief of the Army and Navy, in a time of actual armed rebellion against the authority of the Government of the United States, as a fit and necessary war measure for suppressing said rebellion, do, on this FIRST DAY of JANUARY, in the year of our Lord ONE THOUSAND EIGHT HUNDRED and SIXTY-THREE, and in accordance with my purpose so to do, publicly proclaimed from the date of the first above mentioned order, designate as the States and parts of States therein, the people whereof respectively are this day in rebellion against the United States, the following, to-wit: ARKANSAS, TEXAS, LOUISIANA, except the Parishes of St. Bernard, Plaquemine, Jefferson, St. John, St. Charles, St. James, Ascension, Assumption, Terrebonne, La Fourche, St. Mary, St. Martin, and Orleans, including the city of New Orleans; MISSISSIPPI, ALABAMA, FLORIDA, GEORGIA, SOUTH CAROLINA, NORTH CAROLINA, and VIRGINIA, except the forty-eight counties designated as West Virginia, and also the counties of Berkley, Accomac, Northampton, Elizabeth City, York, Princess Anne, and Norfolk, including the cities of Norfolk and Portsmouth; which excepted parts are for the present left precisely as if this proclamation were not issued. And by virtue of the power and for the purpose aforesaid, I DO ORDER and DECLARE, that ALL PERSONS HELD AS SLAVES within designated States, and parts of States, are, and henceforward SHALL BE FREE, and that the Executive Government of the United States, including the military and naval authorities thereof, will recognize and maintain the freedom of the said persons; and I hereby enjoin upon the people so declared to be free to abstain from all violence, unless in necessary self-defence, and I recommend to them that, in all cases where allowed, they LABOR FAITHFULLY for REASONABLE WAGES; and I further declare and make known that such persons of suitable condition will be received into the armed service of the UNITED STATES, to GARRISON FORTS, POSITIONS, STATIONS, and other places, and to man VESSELS, of all sorts in said service.

And upon this, sincerely believed to be an AN ACT OF JUSTICE, WARRANTED by the CONSTITUTION, upon military necessity, I invoke the CONSIDERATE judgment of MANKIND and the GRACIOUS FAVOR of ALMIGHTY GOD.

In witness whereof, I have hereunto set my hand and caused the seal of the United States, to be affixed. Done at the CITY OF WASHINGTON this FIRST DAY of JANUARY, in the year of our Lord ONE THOUSAND EIGHT HUNDRED and SIXTY-THREE, and of the INDEPENDENCE of the UNITED STATES of AMERICA the EIGHTY-SEVENTH.

(Signed)   ABRAHAM LINCOLN.

By the President:
WM. H. SEWARD, Secretary of State.

THE GETTYSBURG ADDRESS

Abraham Lincoln, 1863

National Cemetery, Gettysburg, Pennsylvania. © G. Ahrens/H. Armstrong Roberts (KH-12300).

Four score and seven years ago our fathers brought forth on this continent, a new nation, conceived in liberty, and dedicated to the proposition that all men are created equal.

Now we are engaged in a great civil war, testing whether that nation or any nation so conceived and so dedicated, can long endure. We are met on a great battle-field of that war. We have come to dedicate a portion of that field, as a final resting place for those who here gave their lives that that nation might live. It is altogether fitting and proper that we should do this.

But, in a larger sense, we can not dedicate—we can not consecrate—we can not hallow—this ground. The brave men, living and dead, who struggled here, have consecrated it, far above our poor power to add or detract. The world will little note, nor long remember what we say here, but it can never forget what they did here. It is for us the living, rather, to be dedicated here to the unfinished work which they who fought here have thus far so nobly advanced. It is rather for us to be here dedicated to the great task remaining before us—that from these honored dead we take increased devotion to that cause for which they gave the last full measure of devotion—that we here highly resolved that these dead shall not have died in vain—that this nation, under God, shall have a new birth of freedom—and that government of the people, by the people, for the people, shall not perish from the earth.

FREEDOM FOR ALL

FREEDOM
for All

I do the very best I know how—the very best I can; and I mean to keep doing so until the end. If the end brings me out all right, what is said against me won't amount to anything. If the end brings me out wrong, ten angels swearing I was right would make no difference.

—ABRAHAM LINCOLN

"FREE AT LAST! FREE AT LAST! THANK GOD ALMIGHTY, WE ARE FREE AT LAST!"

—MARTIN LUTHER KING, JR.

We are coming, Father Abraham, three hundred thousand more,
From Mississippi's winding stream and from New England's shore;
We leave our plows and workshops, our wives and children dear,
With hearts too full for utterance, with but a silent tear;
We dare not look behind us, but steadfastly before:
We are coming, Father Abraham, three hundred thousand more!

You have called us, and we're coming, by Richmond's bloody tide
To lay us down, for Freedom's sake, our brothers' bones beside,
Or from foul treason's savage grasp to wrench the murderous blade,
And in the face of foreign foes its fragments to parade.
Six hundred thousand loyal men and true have gone before:
We are coming, Father Abraham, three hundred thousand more!

—JAMES SLOAN GIBBONS

80

TO MRS. BIXBY, BOSTON, MASS.

Dear Madam, I have been shown in the files of the War Department . . . that you are the mother of five sons who have died gloriously on the field of battle. I feel how weak and fruitless must be any word of mine which should attempt to beguile you from the grief of a loss so overwhelming. But I cannot refrain from tendering you the consolation that may be found in the thanks of the republic they died to save. I pray that our Heavenly Father may assuage the anguish of your bereavement, and leave you only the cherished memory of the loved and lost, and the solemn pride that must be yours to have laid so costly a sacrifice upon the altar of freedom.

—A. LINCOLN, 1864

My Friends: No one, not in my situation, can appreciate my feeling of sadness at this parting. To this place, and the kindness of these people, I owe everything. . . . I now leave, not knowing when or whether ever I may return, with a task before me greater than that which rested upon Washington. Without the assistance of that Divine Being who ever attended him, I cannot succeed. With that assistance, I cannot fail. Trusting in Him who can go with me, and remain with you, and be everywhere for good, let us confidently hope that all will yet be well. To His care commending you, as I hope in your prayers you will commend me, I bid you an affectionate farewell.

—ABRAHAM LINCOLN

SECOND INAUGURAL ADDRESS

Abraham Lincoln, 1865

LINCOLN AT INDEPENDENCE HALL by Jean Leon Gerome Ferris, 1863-1930. © SuperStock (900-122814).

On the occasion corresponding to this four years ago all thoughts were anxiously directed to an impending civil war. All dreaded it, all sought to avert it. While the inaugural address was being delivered from this place, devoted altogether to saving the Union without war, insurgent agents were in the city seeking to destroy it without war—seeking to dissolve the Union and divide effects by negotiation. Both parties deprecated war, but one of them would make war rather than let the nation survive, and the other would accept war rather than let it perish, and the war came. . . .

Neither party expected for the war the magnitude or the duration which it has already attained. . . . Both read the same Bible and pray to the same God, and each invokes His aid against the other. It may seem strange that any men should dare to ask a just God's assistance in wringing their bread from the sweat of other men's faces, but let us judge not, that we be not judged. The prayers of both could not be answered. That of neither has been answered fully. The Almighty has His own purposes. "Woe unto the world because of offenses; for it must needs be that offenses come, but woe to that man by whom the offense cometh." If we shall suppose that American slavery is one of those offenses which, in the providence of God, must needs come, but which, having continued through His appointed time, He now wills to remove, and that He gives to both North and South this terrible war as the woe due to those by whom the offense came, shall we discern therein any departure from those divine attributes which the believers in a living God always ascribe to Him? Fondly do we hope, fervently do we pray, that this mighty scourge of war may speedily pass away. Yet, if God wills that it continue until all the wealth piled by the bondsman's two hundred and fifty years of unrequited toil shall be sunk, and until every drop of blood drawn with the lash shall be paid by another drawn with the sword; as was said three thousand years ago, so still it must

be said "the judgments of the Lord are true and righteous altogether."

 With malice toward none, with charity for all, with firmness in the right as God gives us to see the right, let us strive on to finish the work we are in, to bind up the nation's wounds, to care for him who shall have borne the battle and for his widow and his orphan, to do all which may achieve and cherish a just and lasting peace among ourselves and with all nations.

INAUGURAL ADDRESS

John F. Kennedy, 1961

We observe today not a victory of party but a celebration of freedom—symbolizing an end as well as a beginning, signifying renewal as well as change. For I have sworn before you and Almighty God the same solemn oath our forebears prescribed nearly a century and three-quarters ago.

The world is very different now. For man holds in his mortal hands the power to abolish all forms of human poverty and all forms of human life. And yet the same revolutionary beliefs for which our forebears fought are still at issue around the globe: the belief that the rights of man come not from the generosity of the state but from the hand of God.

We dare not forget today that we are the heirs of that first revolution. Let the word go forth from this time and place, to friend and foe alike, that the torch has been passed to a new generation of Americans—born in this century, tempered by war, disciplined by a hard and bitter peace, proud of our ancient heritage—and unwilling to witness or permit the slow undoing of those human rights to which this nation has always been committed, and to which we are committed today at home and around the world.

Let every nation know, whether it wishes us well or ill, that we shall pay any price, bear any burden, meet any hardship, support any friend, oppose any foe to assure the survival and the success of liberty.

This much we pledge . . . .

Fireworks over the Lincoln Memorial, Washington, D.C. © Ferrell McCollough/SuperStock (1339-101).

MARCH ON WASHINGTON ADDRESS

Martin Luther King, Jr.
1963

Civil Rights Memorial, Montgomery, Alabama, designed by Maya Lin. Photo © Southern Poverty Law Center.

I say to you today, my friends, that in spite of the difficulties and frustrations of the moment I still have a dream. It is a dream deeply rooted in the American dream.

I have a dream that one day this nation will rise up and live out the true meaning of its creed: "We hold these truths to be self-evident; that all men are created equal."

I have a dream that one day on the red hills of Georgia the sons of former slaves and the sons of former slave owners will be able to sit down together at the table of brotherhood.

I have a dream that one day even the state of Mississippi, a desert state sweltering with the heat of injustice and oppression, will be transformed into an oasis of freedom and justice.

I have a dream that my four little children will one day live in a nation where they will not be judged by the color of their skin but by the content of their character.

I have a dream today.

I have a dream that one day the state of Alabama, whose governor's lips are presently dripping with the words of interposition and nullification, will be transformed into a situation where little black boys and black girls will be able to join hands with little white boys and girls and walk together as sisters and brothers.

I have a dream today.

I have a dream that one day every valley shall be exalted, every hill and mountain shall be made low, the rough places will be made plain, and the crooked places will be made straight, and the glory of the Lord shall be revealed, and all flesh shall see it together. . . .

With this faith we will be able to work together, to pray together, to struggle together, to go to jail together, to stand up for freedom together, knowing that we will be free one day.

This will be the day when all of God's children will be able to sing

with new meaning, "My country 'tis of thee, sweet land of liberty, of thee I sing. Land where my father died, land of the Pilgrims' pride, from every mountainside, let freedom ring."

And if America is to be a great nation, this must become true. So let freedom ring from the prodigious hilltops of New Hampshire. Let freedom ring from the mighty mountains of New York. Let freedom ring from the heightening Alleghenies of Pennsylvania! . . .

Let freedom ring from every hill and molehill of Mississippi. From every mountainside, let freedom ring.

When we let freedom ring, when we let it ring from every village and every hamlet, from every state and every city, we will be able to speed up that day when all of God's children, black men and white men, Jews and Gentiles, Protestants and Catholics, will be able to join hands and sing in the words of the old Negro spiritual, "Free at last! Free at last! Thank God Almighty, we are free at last!"

87

KNOW'ST THOU AMERICA

VICTOR E. SOUTHWORTH

Know'st thou America, where we from every land
Unite in friendly fellowship, all evil to withstand?
Where freedom of the people forever reigns supreme?
Where we together labor to render real our dream?

Know'st thou America? We call the world to see
The greatness of America that is and is to be.
Know'st thou the glory of what we can achieve
When we for one another in liberty believe?

When human worth stands foremost, the chiefest of all good,
And democratic principle is clearly understood?
Know'st thou America? With spirit unconfined
In joyous self-surrender we stand for humankind!

Statue of Liberty on the Fourth of July, New York, New
York. © H. Armstrong Roberts (KR-128301).

INAUGURAL ADDRESS

Lyndon B. Johnson

JANUARY 20, 1965

A meandering stream flows toward a ranch on Antelope Flats with the Teton Peaks in the rosy glow of daybreak. Grand Teton National Park, Wyoming. © Terry Donnelly (WYTN322.03.4.Y).

O n this occasion the oath I have taken before you and before God is not mine alone, but ours together. We are one nation and one people. Our fate as a nation and our future as a people rest not upon one citizen but upon all citizens. That is the majesty and the meaning of this moment. . . .

They came here—the exile and the stranger, brave but frightened—to find a place where a man could be his own man. They made a covenant with this land. Conceived in justice, written in liberty, bound in union, it was meant one day to inspire the hopes of all mankind. And it binds us still. If we keep its terms we shall flourish. . . .

First, justice was the promise that all who made the journey would share in the fruits of the land. . . . Justice requires us to remember: when any citizen denies his fellow, saying, "His color is not mine or his beliefs are strange and different," in that moment he betrays America, though his forebears created this nation. . . .

Under this covenant of justice, liberty, and union we have become a nation—prosperous, great, and mighty. And we have kept our freedom. But we have no promise from God that our greatness will endure. We have been allowed by Him to seek greatness with the sweat of our hands and the strength of our spirit. . . .

In each generation, with toil and tears, we have had to earn our heritage again. If we fail now then we will have forgotten in abundance what we learned in hardship: that democracy rests on faith, that freedom asks more than it gives, and the judgment of God is harshest on those who are most favored. If we succeed it will not be because of what we have, but it will be because of what we are; not because of what we own, but rather because of what we believe.

For we are a nation of believers. Underneath the clamor of building and the rush of our day's pursuits, we are believers in justice and lib-

erty and in our own union. We believe that every man must someday be free. And we believe in ourselves.

For this is what America is all about. It is the uncrossed desert and the unclimbed ridge. It is the star that is not reached and the harvest that is sleeping in the unplowed ground. Is our world gone? We say farewell. Is a new world coming? We welcome it, and we will bend it to the hopes of man. . . . For myself, I ask only in the words of an ancient leader: "Give me now wisdom and knowledge, that I may go out and come in before this people: for who can judge this thy people, that is so great?"

91

BATTLE HYMN OF THE REPUBLIC

JULIA WARD HOWE

Mine eyes have seen the glory of the coming of the Lord;
He is trampling out the vintage where the grapes of wrath are stored;
He hath loosed the fateful lightning of His terrible swift sword:
    His truth is marching on.

I have seen Him in the watch fires of a hundred circling camps;
They have builded Him an altar in the evening dews and damps;
I can read His righteous sentence by the dim and flaring lamps:
    His day is marching on.

I have read a fiery gospel writ in burnished rows of steel:
"As ye deal with my contemners, so with you my grace shall deal;
Let the Hero, born of woman, crush the serpent with his heel,
    Since God is marching on."

He has sounded forth the trumpet that shall never call retreat;
He is sifting out the hearts of men before His judgment seat:
Oh, be swift, my soul, to answer Him! Be jubilant, my feet!
    Our God is marching on.

In the beauty of the lilies Christ was born across the sea,
With a glory in his bosom that transfigures you and me:
As he died to make men holy, let us die to make men free,
    While God is marching on.

Lincoln Memorial, Washington, D.C. © Tim
Hursley/SuperStock (840-358A).

THE NEW COLOSSUS

EMMA LAZARUS

Not like the brazen giant of Greek fame,
With conquering limbs astride from land to land;
Here at our sea-washed, sunset gates shall stand
A mighty woman with a torch, whose flame
Is the imprisoned lightning, and her name
Mother of Exiles. From her beacon-hand
Glows world-wide welcome; her mild eyes command
The air-bridged harbor that twin cities frame.

"Keep, ancient lands, your storied pomp!" cries she
With silent lips. "Give me your tired, your poor,
Your huddled masses yearning to breathe free,
The wretched refuse of your teeming shore.
Send these, the homeless, tempest-tost to me,
I lift my lamp beside the golden door!"

Ellis Island, New York City, New York. © Steve
Vidler/SuperStock (1288-901).

United States Marine Corps War
Memorial, Arlington, Virginia. © Ferrell
McCollough/SuperStock (1339-148A)

DEFENDING
THE
FAITH

THE IDEALS TREASURY OF FAITH IN AMERICA

THE SPIRIT OF LIBERTY

JUDGE LEARNED HAND, 1944

What then is the spirit of liberty?
I cannot define it; I can only tell you of my own faith.

The spirit of liberty is the spirit which is not too sure that it is right;
the spirit of liberty is the spirit which seeks to understand the minds
      of other men and women;
the spirit of liberty is the spirit which weighs their interests
      alongside its own without bias;
the spirit of liberty remembers that not even a sparrow
      falls to earth unheeded;
the spirit of liberty is the spirit of Him who, near two thousand years ago,
      taught mankind that lesson it has never learned, but has never quite
      forgotten; that there may be a kingdom where the least shall be
      heard and considered side by side with the greatest.

And now in that spirit, that spirit of an America
      which has never been, and which may never be;
      nay, which never will be except as the conscience and
      courage of Americans create it;
yet in the spirit of that America
      which lies hidden in some form in the aspirations of us all;
in the spirit of that America
      for which our young men are at this moment fighting and dying;
in that spirit of liberty and of America
      I ask you to rise and with me pledge our faith in the glorious
      destiny of our beloved country.

Washington Monument, Washington, D.C. © Ferrell
McCollough/SuperStock (1399-144A).

DEFENDING
Liberty

These are the times that try men's souls: The summer soldier and the sunshine patriot will in this crisis, shrink from the service of his country; but he that stands it now, deserves the love and thanks of man and woman. Tyranny, like hell, is not easily conquered; yet we have this consolation with us, that the harder the conflict, the more glorious the triumph. What we obtain too cheap, we esteem too lightly.

—THOMAS PAINE

I believe in the United States of America as a government of the people, for the people, by the people; whose just powers are derived from the consent of the governed; a democracy in a republic; a sovereign nation of many sovereign states; a perfect union, one and inseparable; established upon those principles of freedom, equality, justice, and humanity for which American patriots sacrificed their lives and fortunes.

I therefore believe it is my duty to my country to love it; to support its Constitution; to obey its laws; to respect its flag; and to defend it against all enemies.

—WILLIAM TYLER PAGE

FROM EARTH
TO HEAVEN I
SALUTE YOU,
MY DEAR AND
FAITHFUL SON.
—JULIE MCPHILLIPS

100

It is not merely for today but for all time to come that we should perpetuate for our children's children that great and free government which we have enjoyed all our lives. I beg you to remember this, not merely for my sake, but for yours. I happen, temporarily, to occupy the White House. I am a living witness that any one of your children may look to come here as my father's child has. It is in order that each one of you may have, through this free government which we have enjoyed, an open field and a fair chance for your industry, enterprise, and intelligence that you may all have equal privileges in the race of life, with all its desirable human aspirations. It is for this the struggle should be maintained that we may not lose our birthright—not only for one, but for two or three years. The nation is worth fighting for to secure such an inestimable jewel.

—ABRAHAM LINCOLN

You are called upon to found a new navy; to lay the foundations of a new power afloat that must some time . . . become formidable enough to dispute even with England the mastery of the ocean. Neither you nor I may live to see such growth. But we are here at the planting of the tree and maybe some of us must, in the course of destiny, water its feeble and struggling roots with our blood. If so, let it be so!

—JOHN PAUL JONES

I hate war as only a soldier who has lived it can, only as one who has seen its brutality, its futility, its stupidity.

—GENERAL DWIGHT D. EISENHOWER

THE STRENUOUS LIFE

Theodore Roosevelt, 1899

Mount Rushmore
National Memorial,
South Dakota. ©
Gala/SuperStock (191-
2827).

I wish to preach, not the doctrine of ignoble ease, but the doctrine of the strenuous life, the life of toil and effort, of labor and strife; to preach that highest form of success which comes, not to the man who desires mere easy peace, but to the man who does not shrink from danger, from hardship, or from bitter toil, and who out of these wins the splendid ultimate triumph.

A life of slothful ease, a life of that peace which springs merely from lack either of desire or of power to strive after great things, is as little worthy of a nation as an individual. I ask only that what every self-respecting American demands from himself and from his sons shall be demanded of the American nation as a whole. Who among you would teach your boys that ease, that peace, is to be the first consideration in their eyes— to be the ultimate goal after which they strive? . . .

We do not admire the man of timid peace. We admire the man who embodies victorious efforts, the man who never wrongs his neighbor, who is prompt to help a friend, but who has those virile qualities necessary to win in the stern strife of actual life. . . .

As it is with the individual, so it is with the nation. It is a base untruth to say that happy is the nation that has no history. Thrice happy is the nation that has a glorious history. Far better it is to dare mighty things, to win glorious triumphs, even though checkered by failure, than to take rank with those poor spirits who neither enjoy much nor suffer much, because they live in the gray twilight that knows neither victory nor defeat. . . .

Let us, the children of the men who proved themselves equal to the mighty days—let us, the children of the men who carried the great civil war to a triumphant conclusion, praise the God of our fathers that the ignoble counsels of peace were rejected; that the suffering and loss, the blackness of sorrow and despair, were unflinchingly faced and the years of strife endured; for in the end the slave was free, the Union restored, and the mighty American Republic placed once more as a helmeted queen among nations.

The Last Message from the Alamo

William Barret Travis, 1836

To the people of Texas and all Americans in the world. Fellow citizens and compatriots: I am besieged by a thousand or more of the Mexicans under Santa Anna. I have sustained a continual bombardment and cannonade for twenty-four hours and have not lost a man. The enemy has demanded a surrender at discretion; otherwise the garrison are to be put to the sword if the fort is taken. I have answered the demand with a cannon shot, and our flag still waves proudly from the walls.

I shall never surrender nor retreat.

I call on you in the name of liberty, of patriotism, and everything dear to the American character, to come to our aid with all dispatch. The enemy is receiving reinforcements daily and will no doubt increase to three or four thousand in four or five days. If this call is neglected, I am determined to sustain myself as long as possible and die like a soldier who never forgets what is due to his own honor and that of our country. VICTORY OR DEATH.

Alamo Mission in San Antonio, Texas. © R. Kord/H. Armstrong Roberts (KR-93101-f).

104

THE BATTLE CRY OF FREEDOM

GEORGE F. ROOT

Yes, we'll rally round the flag, boys, we'll rally once again,
Shouting the battle cry of Freedom,
We'll rally from the hillside, we'll gather from the plain,
Shouting the battle cry of Freedom!

The Union forever, hurrah! boys, hurrah!
Down with the traitor, up with the star,
While we rally round the flag, boys, rally once again,
Shouting the battle cry of Freedom!

We are springing to the call of our brothers gone before,
Shouting the battle cry of Freedom,
And we'll fill the vacant ranks with a million freemen more,
Shouting the battle cry of Freedom!

We will welcome to our numbers the loyal, true, and brave,
Shouting the battle cry of Freedom;
And although they may be poor, not a man shall be a slave,
Shouting the battle cry of Freedom!

So we're springing to the call from the East and from the West,
Shouting the battle cry of Freedom;
And we'll hurl the rebel crew from the land we love the best,
Shouting the battle cry of Freedom!

Parade of American flags. © Pixtal/SuperStock (1436R-150009).

THE SURRENDER OF GENERAL ROBERT E. LEE

Ulysses S. Grant

LET US HAVE PEACE, GRANT AND LEE by Jean Leon Gerome Ferris 1963-1930. © SuperStock (900-4749).

108

What General Lee's feelings were I do not know. As he was a man of much dignity, with an impassible face, it was impossible to say whether he felt inwardly glad that the end had finally come, or felt sad over the result, and was too manly to show it. Whatever his feelings, they were entirely concealed from my observation; but my own feelings, which had been quite jubilant on the receipt of his letter, were sad and depressed. I felt like anything rather than rejoicing at the downfall of a foe who had fought so long and valiantly.

General Lee was dressed in a full uniform which was entirely new, and was wearing a sword of considerable value, very likely the sword which had been presented by the State of Virginia; at all events, it was an entirely different sword from the one that would ordinarily be worn in the field. In my rough traveling suit, the uniform of a private with the straps of a lieutenant-general, I must have contrasted very strangely with a man so handsomely dressed, six feet high and of faultless form. But this was not a matter that I thought of until afterwards.

We soon fell into a conversation about old army times. . . . Our conversation grew so pleasant that I almost forgot the object of our meeting. After the conversation had run on in this style for some time, General Lee called my attention to the object of our meeting, and said he had asked for this interview for the purpose of getting from me the terms I had proposed to give his army. I said that I meant merely that his army should lay down its arms, not to take them up again during the continuance of the war unless duly and properly exchanged. He said that he had so understood my letter. . . .

When news of the surrender first reached our lines our men commenced firing a salute of a hundred guns in honor of the victory. I at once sent word, however, to have it stopped. The Confederates were now our prisoners, and we did not want to exult over their downfall.

WEST POINT CADET'S PRAYER

Clayton E. Wheat

O God, our Father, Thou Searcher of hearts, help us to draw near to Thee in sincerity and truth. May our religion be filled with gladness and may our worship of Thee be natural.

Strengthen and increase our admiration for honest dealing and clean thinking, and suffer not our hatred of hypocrisy and pretense ever to diminish. Encourage us in our endeavor to live above the common level of life. Make us to choose the harder right instead of the easier wrong, and never to be content with a half truth when the whole can be won.

Endow us with courage that is born of loyalty to all that is noble and worthy, that scorns to compromise with vice and injustice and knows no fear when truth and right are in jeopardy. Guard us against flippancy and irreverence in the sacred things of life. Grant us new ties of friendship and new opportunities of service.

Kindle our hearts in fellowship with those of a cheerful countenance, and soften our hearts with sympathy for those who sorrow and suffer. Help us to maintain the honor of the Corps untarnished and unsullied and to show forth in our lives the ideals of West Point in doing our duty to Thee and to our Country. all of which we ask in the name of the Great Friend and Master of mankind.

Amen.

Full-Dress Parade, West Point Military Academy, West Point, New York. © David Forbet/SuperStock (2050-1235).

110

DUTY—HONOR—
COUNTRY

General Douglas MacArthur

1962

Flag of the United States of America. © Emmanuel Faure/SuperStock (46-1639A).

T
he soldier, above all other men, is required to practice the greatest act of religious training—sacrifice. In battle and in the face of danger and death, he discloses those divine attributes which his Maker gave when He created man in His own image. No physical courage and no brute instinct can take the place of the divine help which alone can sustain him. . . .

And through all this welter of change and development, your mission remains fixed, determined, inviolable—it is to win our wars. Everything else in your professional career is but a corollary to this vital dedication. . . . Yours is the profession of arms—the will to win, the sure knowledge that in war there is no substitute for victory; that if you lose, the nation will be destroyed; that the very obsession of your public service must be Duty—Honor—Country.

You stand as the nation's war guardian, as its life-guard from the raging tides of international conflict, as its gladiator in the arena of battle. For a century and a half you have defended, guarded, and protected its hallowed tradition of liberty and freedom, of right and justice. Let civilian voices argue the merits or demerits of our justice. Let civilian voices argue the merits or demerits of our processes of government. . . . These great national problems are not for your professional participation or military solution. Your guidepost stands out like a ten-fold beacon in the night—Duty—Honor—Country.

The long Grey Line has never failed us. Were you to do so, a million ghosts in olive drab, in brown khaki, in blue and gray, would rise from their white crosses thundering those magic words—Duty—Honor—Country.

The soldier, above all other people, prays for peace, for he must suffer and bear the deepest wounds and scars of war. But always in our ears ring the ominous words of Plato, that wisest of all philosophers: "Only the dead have seen the end of War."

The shadows are lengthening for me. The twilight is here. My days of old have vanished tone and tint; they have gone glimmering through the dreams of things that were. Their memory is one of wondrous beauty, watered by tears and coaxed and caressed by the smiles of yesterday.

I listen vainly, but with thirsty ear, for the witching melody of faint bugles blowing reveille, of far drums beating the long roll. In my dreams I hear again the crash of guns, the rattle of musketry, the strange, mournful mutter of the battlefield.

But in the evening of my memory, always I come back to West Point. Always there echoes and re-echoes Duty—Honor—Country.

Today marks my final roll call with you, but I want you to know that when I cross the river, my last conscious thought will be The Corps—and The Corps—and The Corps.

I bid you farewell.

WAR MESSAGE

Woodrow Wilson, 1917

It is a fearful thing to lead this great peaceful people into war, into the most terrible and disastrous of all wars, civilization itself seeming to be in the balance.

But the right is more precious than peace, and we shall fight for the things which we have always carried nearest our hearts—for democracy, for the right of those who submit to authority to have a voice in their own governments, for the rights and liberties of small nations, for a universal dominion of right by such a concert of free peoples as shall bring peace and safety to all nations and make the world itself at last free. To such a task we can dedicate our lives and our fortunes, everything that we are and everything that we have, with the pride of those who know that the day has come when America is privileged to spend her blood and her might for the principles that gave her birth and happiness and the peace which she has treasured. God helping her, she can do no other.

World War I soldiers' homecoming parade in New York, New York. © Culver Pictures, Inc./ SuperStock (486-232).

114

LAND OF THE FREE

ARTHUR NICHOLAS HOSKING

America, O power benign, great hearts revere your name,
You stretch your hand to every land, to weak and strong the same;
You claim no conquest of the sea, nor conquest of the field,
But conquest for the rights of man, that despots all shall yield.

America, fair land of mine, home of the just and true,
All hail to thee, land of the free, and the red-white-and-blue.
America, staunch, undismayed, your spirit is our might:
No splendor falls on feudal walls upon your mountain's height,
But shafts of justice pierce your skies to light the way for all,
A world's great brotherhood of man, that cannot, must not fall.

America, in God we trust, we fear no tyrant's horde:
There's light that leads toward better deeds than conquest by the sword;
Yet our cause is just, if fight we must until the world be free
Of every menace, inside or out, that strikes at liberty.

America, home of the brave, our song in praise we bring—
Where Stars and Stripes the winds unfurl, 'tis there that tributes ring;
Our fathers gave their lives that we should live in freedom's light—
Our lives we consecrate to thee, our guide the might of right.

America, fair land of mine, home of the just and true,
All hail to thee, land of the free, and the red-white-and-blue.

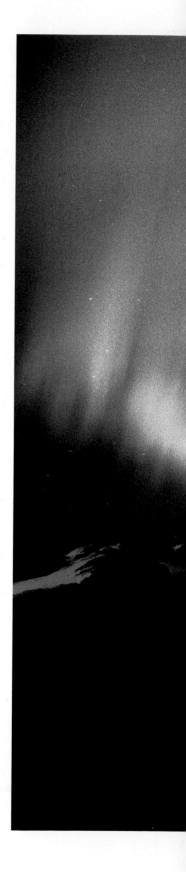

Bald eagle and the Aurora Borealis, Alaska. © Dale
O'Dell/SuperStock (1400-108).

DEFENDING THE FAITH

FROM THE FOUR FREEDOMS SPEECH

Franklin D. Roosevelt, 1941

As men do not live by bread alone, they do not fight by armaments alone. Those who man our defenses, and those behind them who build our defenses, must have the stamina and courage which come from an unshakable belief in the manner of life which they are defending. The mighty action which we are calling for cannot be based on a disregard of all things worth fighting for. . . .

In the future days, which we seek to make secure, we look forward to a world founded upon four essential human freedoms. The first is freedom of speech and expression, everywhere in the world. The second is freedom of every person to worship God in his own way, everywhere in the world. The third is freedom from want, which, translated into world terms, means economic understandings which will secure to every nation a healthy peacetime life for its inhabitants, everywhere in the world.

The fourth is freedom from fear—which, translated into world terms, means a worldwide reduction of armaments to such a point and in such a thorough fashion that no nation will be in a position to commit an act of physical aggression against any neighbor—anywhere in the world.

That is no vision of a distant millennium. It is a definite basis for a kind of world attainable in our own time and generation. That kind of world is the very antithesis of the so-called "new order" of tyranny which the dictators seek to create with the crash of a bomb.

To that new order we oppose the greater conception—the moral order. A good society is able to face schemes of world domination and foreign revolutions alike without fear.

Since the beginning of our American history we have been engaged in change—in a perpetual peaceful revolution, a revolution which goes on steadily, quietly adjusting itself to changing conditions, without the concentration camp or the quick lime in the ditch. The world order which we seek is the cooperation of free countries, working together in a friendly, civilized society.

FREEDOM TO WORSHIP
by Norman Rockwell.
Copyright © 1943 the
Norman Rockwell
Family Entities.

118

EACH ACCORDING TO THE DICTATES OF HIS OWN CONSCIENCE

NORMAN ROCKWELL

This nation has placed its destiny in the hands and heads and hearts of its millions of free men and women, and its faith in freedom under the guidance of God. Freedom means the supremacy of human rights everywhere. Our support goes to those who struggle to gain those rights or keep them. Our strength is in our unity of purpose.

To that high concept there can be no end save victory.

119

PRAYER

Peter Marshall, 1947

Vietnam Veterans Memorial, Washington, D.C. © Joanna McCarthy/SuperStock (1336-344).

God of our fathers, whose almighty hand hath made and preserved our nation, grant that our people may understand what it is they celebrate tomorrow.

May they remember how bitterly our freedom was won, the down payment that was made for it, the installments that have been made since this republic was born, and the price that must yet be paid for our liberty.

May freedom be seen not as the right to do as we please but as the opportunity to please to do what is right. May it ever be understood that our liberty is under God and can be found nowhere else. May our faith be something that is not merely stamped upon our coins but expressed in our lives.

Let us, as a nation, not be afraid of standing alone for the rights of men, since we were born that way, as the only nation on earth that came into being "for the glory of God and the advancement of the Christian faith." We know that we shall be true to the Pilgrim dream when we are true to the God they worshiped.

To the extent that America honors thee, wilt thou bless America, and keep her true as thou hast kept her free, and make her good as thou hast made her rich. Amen

D C HOPEWLL • ALBRT L HORNR •
N I JACKSON • JAMES L JAKO •
AL R KIRBY III • GUY D KISTNER •
EONARD M LEE • JOHN C ROMANSHEK •
ALE • JAMES E LOUDERMILK •
SAMMY A MARTIN • ROBERT T MILLER
PALMA • MICHAEL L PARKER •
T • OSSIE REYNOLDS •
SCHMITZ • GARY R SCHWELLENBACH
CZYK • THOMAS N STILES •
ANLIN WEBSTER • JAMES E WILLIAM
NTILL • ROBERT L BOYER •
CARL E CHAMBERLAIN • JOHN G C
SER • BYRON A GAINES Jr •
RNANDEZ • THOMAS B HOLDBRO
D A NIEDECKEN • JUAN ORTIZ-RIV
J STRECKERT • ERNESTO TARANG
NNIE H BEALS • DAVID A BLOUC
OVINGTON • CARLOS R CRUZ
DOYLE • WAYNE A ECKLEY •
M • KEVIN B HARDIMAN • JOSE
NSON • ROBERT H McWILLIAM
DEN • JACK McCRARY •
ROSSI Jr • WILLIAM J POTTER Jr
MITH • GERALD G VAN BUREN

THE IDEALS TREASURY OF FAITH IN AMERICA

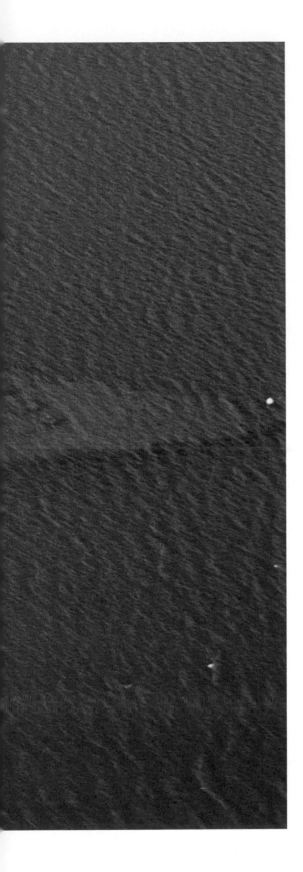

NAVY HYMN

WILLIAM WHITING

Eternal Father, strong to save,
Whose arm hath bound the restless wave,
Who bidd'st the mighty ocean deep
Its own appointed limits keep,
Oh, hear us when we cry to thee
For those in peril on the sea!

O Christ, whose voice the waters heard
And hushed their raging at thy word,
Who walked on the foaming deep
And calm amidst its rage didst sleep,
Oh, hear us when we cry to thee
For those in peril on the sea!

Most Holy Spirit, who didst brood
Upon the chaos dark and rude
And bid its angry tumult cease
And give, for wild confusion, peace,
Oh, hear us when we cry to thee
For those in peril on the sea!

The USS *Arizona* Memorial lies over the sunken battle-
ship by the same name in Pearl Harbor, Hawaii. © H.
Armstrong Roberts (KR-120235-g).

GENERAL EISENHOWER'S D DAY ORDER OF THE DAY

Dwight D. Eisenhower

JUNE 6, 1944

United States Cemetery Saint Laurent Normandie, France. © K. Scholz/ H. Armstrong Roberts (087188).

Soldiers, sailors, and airmen of the Allied expeditionary force: You are about to embark upon a great crusade toward which we have striven these many months. The eyes of the world are upon you. The hopes and prayers of liberty-loving peoples everywhere march with you.

You will bring about the destruction of the German war machine, the elimination of Nazi tyranny over the oppressed peoples of Europe, and security for ourselves in a free world. Your task will not be an easy one. Your enemy is well-trained, well-equipped, and battle-hardened. He will fight savagely. But this is the year 1944. Much has happened since the Nazi triumphs of 1940–41. . . .

Our home fronts have given us an overwhelming superiority in weapons and munitions of war and placed at our disposal great reserves of trained fighting men.

The tide has turned. The free men of the world are marching together to victory. I have full confidence in your courage, devotion to duty, and skill in battle. We will accept nothing less than full victory.

Good luck, and let us all beseech the blessings of Almighty God upon this great and noble undertaking.

125

FOR PEACE AND UNITY

FRANKLIN DELANO ROOSEVELT

Almighty God . . . With thy blessing, we shall prevail over the forces of our enemy. . . . Lead us to be the saving of our country, and with our sister nations into a world unity that will spell a sure peace—a peace invulnerable to the schemings of unworthy men. And a peace that will let all men live in freedom, reaping the just rewards of honest toil.

Thy will be done, Almighty God.

Amen.

FLANDERS FIELD

JOHN MCCRAE

In Flanders Fields the poppies blow
Between the crosses, row on row,
That mark our place; and in the sky
The larks, still bravely singing, fly
Scarce heard amid the guns below.
To you from failing hands we throw

Take up your quarrel with the foe!
To you from failing hands, we throw
The torch—Be yours to hold it high!
If ye break faith with us who die
We shall not sleep, though poppies grow
      In Flanders Fields.

Military headstones in Arlington National Cemetary,
Arlington, Virginia. © Bruce Dorrier/SuperStock (113-341).

INAUGURAL ADDRESS

Harry S Truman

JANUARY 20, 1949

E ach period of our national history has had its special challenges. Those that confront us now are as momentous as any in the past. Today marks the beginning not only of a new administration, but of a period that will be eventful, perhaps decisive, for us and for the world. . . .

It is fitting, therefore, that we take this occasion to proclaim to the world the essential principles of the faith by which we live, and to declare our aims to all peoples. The American people stand firm in the faith which has inspired this nation from the beginning. We believe that all men have a right to equal justice under law and equal opportunity to share in the common good. We believe that all men have a right to freedom of thought and expression. We believe that all men are created equal because they are created in the image of God. From this faith we will not be moved.

The American people desire, and are determined to work for, a world in which all nations and all peoples are free to govern themselves as they see fit, and to achieve a decent and satisfying life. Above all else, our people desire, and are determined to work for, peace on earth—a just and lasting peace—based on genuine agreement freely arrived at by equals. . . . To that end we will devote our strength, our resources, and our firmness of resolve. With God's help, the future of mankind will be assured in a world of justice, harmony, and peace.

The sun shines through the trees, in rural Virginia. © Dick Dietrich (VAX-08766.00)

THE KOREAN ARMISTICE

Dwight D. Eisenhower

JULY 26, 1953

Military guard at the Tomb of the Unknown Soldier, Arlington, Virginia. © Murat Ayranci/SuperStock (1131-169).

My Fellow Citizens: Tonight we greet, with prayers of thanksgiving, the official news that an armistice was signed almost an hour ago in Korea. It will quickly bring to an end the fighting between the United Nations forces and the Communist armies. For this nation, the cost of repelling aggression has been high. In thousands of homes it has been incalculable. It has been paid in terms of tragedy.

With special feelings of sorrow—and of solemn gratitude—we think of those who were called upon to lay down their lives in that far-off land to prove once again that only courage and sacrifice can keep freedom alive upon the earth. To the widows and orphans of this war, and to those veterans who bear disabling wounds, America renews tonight her pledge of lasting devotion and care.

Soldiers, sailors, and airmen of sixteen different countries have stood as partners beside us throughout these long and bitter months. America's thanks go to each. In this struggle we have seen the United Nations meet the challenge of aggression—not with pathetic words of protest, but with deeds of decisive purpose. . . .

And so at long last the carnage of war is to cease and the negotiation of the conference table is to begin. On this Sabbath evening each of us devoutly prays that all nations may come to see the wisdom of composing differences in this fashion before, rather than after, there is resort to brutal and futile battle.

Now as we strive to bring about that wisdom, there is, in this moment of sober satisfaction, one thought that must discipline our emotions and steady our resolution. It is this: We have won an armistice on a single battleground—not peace in the world. We may not now relax our guard nor cease our quest. . . . We shall fervently strive to insure that this armistice will, in fact, bring free people one step nearer to a goal of a world of peace.

130

DEFENDING THE FAITH

FIRST INAUGURAL ADDRESS

Ronald Reagan

JANUARY 20, 1981

The White House in Washington, D.C. © SuperStock (40-11481A).

To a few of us here today this is a solemn and most momentous occasion, and yet in the history of our nation it is a commonplace occurrence. The orderly transfer of authority as called for in the Constitution routinely takes place, as it has for almost two centuries, and few of us stop to think how unique we really are. In the eyes of many in the world, this every-four-year-ceremony we accept as normal is nothing less than a miracle. . . .

I'm told that tens of thousands of prayer meetings are being held on this day, and for that I'm deeply grateful. We are a nation under God, and I believe God intended for us to be free. It would be fitting and good, I think, if on each inaugural day in future years it should be declared a day of prayer.

This is the first time in our history that this ceremony has been held, as you've been told, on this west front of the Capitol. Standing here, one faces a magnificent vista, opening up on this city's special beauty and history. At the end of this open mall are those shrines to the giants on whose shoulders we stand.

Directly in front of me, the monument to a monumental man, George Washington, father of our country—a man of humility who came to greatness reluctantly. He led America out of revolutionary victory into infant nationhood. Off to one side, the stately memorial to Thomas Jefferson. The Declaration of Independence flames with his eloquence. And then, beyond the Reflecting Pool, the dignified columns of the Lincoln Memorial. Whoever would understand in his heart the meaning of America will find it in the life of Abraham Lincoln.

Beyond those monuments to heroism is the Potomac River, and on the far shore the sloping hills of Arlington National Cemetery, with its row upon row of simple white markers. . . . They add up to only a tiny fraction of the price that has been paid for our freedom.

Each one of those markers is a monument to the kind of hero I spoke of earlier. Their lives ended in places called Belleau Wood, the Argonne, Omaha Beach, Salerno, and halfway around the world on Guadalcanal, Tarawa, Pork Chop Hill, the Chosin Reservoir, and in a hundred rice paddies and jungles of a place called Vietnam.

Under one such marker lies a young man, Martin Treptow, who left his job in a small town barbershop in 1917 to go to France with the famed Rainbow Division. There, on the western front, he was killed trying to carry a message between battalions under heavy artillery fire.

We're told that on his body was found a diary. On the flyleaf under the heading "My Pledge" he had written these words: "America must win this war. Therefore I will work, I will save, I will sacrifice, I will endure, I will fight cheerfully and do my utmost, as if the issue of the whole struggle depended on me alone."

The crisis we are facing today does not require of us the kind of sacrifice that Martin Treptow and so many thousands of others were called upon to make. It does require, however, our best effort and our willingness to believe in ourselves and to believe in our capacity to perform great deeds, to believe that together with God's help we can and will resolve the problems which now confront us.

And after all, why shouldn't we believe that? We are American.

God bless you, and thank you.

133

LORD, GUARD AND GUIDE THE MEN WHO FLY

MARY C. D. HAMILTON

Lord, guard and guide the men who fly
Through the great spaces of the sky;
Be with them traversing the air
In darkening storms or sunshine fair.

Thou who dost keep with tender might
The balanced birds in all their flight,
Thou of the tempered winds, be near,
That, having thee, they know no fear.

Control their minds with instinct fit
What time, adventuring, they quit
The firm security of land;
Grant steadfast eye and skillful hand.

Aloft in solitudes of space,
Uphold them with thy saving grace.
O God, protect the men who fly
Thru lonely ways beneath the sky.
Amen.

United States Air Force C-141 "Starlifter" takes off into the
sunset. © StockTrek/SuperStock (1457-154).

135

The Lanterns of Faith

John McCain, 1999

Our senior officers always stressed to us the three essential keys to resistance, which we were to keep uppermost in our mind, especially in moments when we were isolated or otherwise deprived of their guidance and the counsel of other prisoners. They were faith in God, faith in country, and faith in your fellow prisoners.

Were your faith in any of these three devotions seriously shaken, you became much more vulnerable to various pressures employed by the Vietnamese to break you. The purpose of our captors' inhumanity to us was nothing less than to force our descent into a world of total faithlessness; a world with no God, no country, no loyalty. Our faith would be replaced with simple reliance on the sufferance of our antagonists. Without faith, we would lose our dignity, and live among our enemies as animals lived among their human masters.

There were times in many a prisoner's existence when the Vietnamese came close to robbing his faith; when a prisoner felt abandoned, left to cling to faith in himself as his last strength, his last form of resistance. Certainly this had been my experience when I was broken in the fall of 1968.

Ironically for someone who had so long asserted his own individuality as his first and best defense against insults of any kind, I discovered that faith in myself proved to be the least formidable strength I possessed when confronting alone organized inhumanity on a greater scale than I had conceived possible. Faith in myself was important, and remains important to my self-esteem. But I discovered in prison that faith in myself alone, separate from other, more important allegiances, was ultimately no match for the cruelty that human beings could devise when they were entirely unencumbered by respect for the God-given dignity of man. This is the lesson I learned in prison. It is, perhaps, the most important lesson I have ever learned.

During the worst moments of captivity, keeping our faith in God, country, and one another was as difficult as it was imperative. When your

Navy pilot boarding his plane on a United States carrier. © E. Masterson/H. Armstrong Roberts (KM-9134-h).

136

faith weakened, you had to take any opportunity, seize on any sight of it, and use any temporary relief from your distress to recover it.

POWs often regard their prison experience as comparable to the trials of Job. Indeed, for my fellow prisoners who suffered more than I, the comparison is appropriate. Hungry, beaten, hurt, scared, and alone, human beings can begin to feel that they are removed from God's love, a vast distance separating them from their Creator. The anguish can lead to resentment, to the awful despair that God has forsaken you.

To guard against such despair, in our most dire moments, POWs would make supreme efforts to grasp our faith tightly, to profess it alone, in the dark, and hasten its revival. Once I was thrown into another cell after a long and difficult interrogation. I discovered scratched into one of the cell's walls the creed "I believe in God, the Father Almighty." There, standing witness to God's presence in a remote, concealed place, recalled to my faith by a stronger, better man, I felt God's love and care more vividly than I would have felt it had I been safe among a congregation in the most magnificent cathedral. . . .

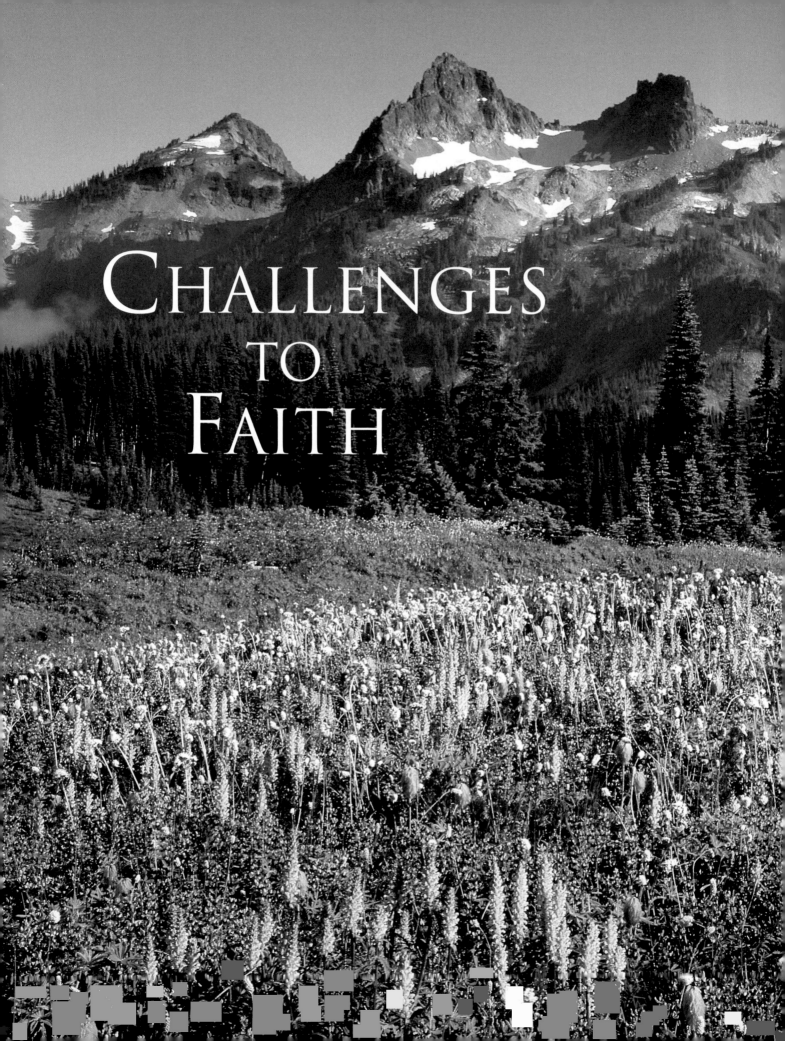

CHALLENGES TO FAITH

Tatoosh mountain range and an alpine wildflower meadow in Mount Rainier National Park, Washington. © Mary Liz Austin (WARN328.15).

Now is the time to take longer strides—time for a great new enterprise—time for this nation to take a clearly leading role in space achievements which, in many ways, may hold the key to our future on earth. . . .

I believe that this nation should commit itself to achieving the goal, before this decade is out, of landing a man on the moon and returning him safely to earth. No single space project in this period will be more impressive to mankind or more important for the long-range exploration of space. And none will be so difficult to accomplish. . . . Let it be clear that this is a judgment which the members of the Congress must finally make. Let it be clear that I am asking the Congress and the country to accept a firm commitment to a new course of action. . . .

I believe we should go to the moon.

FROM A SPEECH TO CONGRESS

John Fitzgerald Kennedy

1961

Fluttering American flag with the moon in the background. © Dennis Frates (FSM 717).

140

CHALLENGES TO FAITH

REMEMBER
faith preserved

This cause of exploration and discovery is not an option we choose; it is a desire written in the human heart. We are that part of creation which seeks to understand all creation. We find the best among us, send them forth into unmapped darkness, and pray they will return. They go in peace for all mankind, and all mankind is in their debt.

—George W. Bush

Faint not,
fight on!
Tomorrow
comes the song.

—Maltbie D. Babcock

While our navy and our airplanes and our guns may be our first lines of defense, it is still clear that way down at the bottom, underlying them all, giving them their strength and sustenance and power, are the spirit and morale of a free people.

—President Franklin D. Roosevelt, 1940

142

God of our fathers, who by land and sea has ever led us to victory, please continue your inspiring guidance in this the greatest of our conflicts. Strengthen my soul so that the weakening instinct of self-preservation, which bests all in battle, shall not blind me in my duty to my responsibility to my fellow soldiers. Grant to our armed forces that disciplined valor and mutual confidence which ensures success in war. Let me not mourn for the men who have died fighting, but rather let me be glad that such heroes have lived. If it be my lot to die, let me do so with courage and honor . . . and please, O Lord, protect and guard those I shall leave behind. Grant us the victory, Lord.

—GENERAL GEORGE S. PATTON, 1944

It is my earnest hope . . . that from this solemn occasion, a better world shall emerge . . . a world dedicated to the dignity of man. . . . Let us pray that peace be restored to the world, and that God will preserve it always.

—GENERAL DOUGLAS MACARTHUR, 1945

Let me assure you that my hand is the steadier for the work that is to be done, that I move more firmly into the task, knowing that you   millions and millions of you   are joined with me in the resolve to make this work endure. . . . And to all Americans who dedicate themselves with us to the making of an abiding peace, I say, The only limit to our realization of tomorrow will be our doubts of today. Let us move forward with strong and active faith.

—PRESIDENT FRANKLIN D. ROOSEVELT, 1945

THE *APOLLO 8* CHRISTMAS EVE BROADCAST

Astronauts Anders, Borman, Lovell, 1968

Earth as viewed from 240,000 miles away in the spacecraft of *Apollo* XI. © H. Armstrong Roberts (KP-3144).

Apollo 8, the first manned mission to the Moon, entered lunar orbit on Christmas Eve, December 24, 1968. That evening, the astronauts: Commander Frank Borman, Command Module Pilot Jim Lovell, and Lunar Module Pilot William Anders did a live television broadcast from lunar orbit, in which they showed pictures of the Earth and Moon seen from *Apollo* 8.

Lovell said, "The vast loneliness is awe-inspiring and it makes you realize just what you have back there on Earth." They ended the broadcast with the crew taking turns reading from the book of Genesis.

WILLIAM ANDERS: "For all the people on Earth, the crew of *Apollo* 8 has a message we would like to send you: 'In the beginning God created the heaven and the earth. And the earth was without form, and void; and darkness was upon the face of the deep.

"'And the Spirit of God moved upon the face of the waters. And God said, Let there be light: and there was light.

"'And God saw the light, that it was good: and God divided the light from the darkness.'"

JIM LOVELL: "'And God called the light Day, and the darkness he called Night. And the evening and the morning were the first day. And God said, Let there be a firmament in the midst of the waters, and let it divide the waters from the waters.

"'And God made the firmament, and divided the waters which were under the firmament from the waters which were above the firmament: and it was so. And God called the firmament Heaven. And the evening and the morning were the second day.'"

FRANK BORMAN: "'And God said, Let the waters under the heavens be gathered together unto one place, and let the dry land appear: and it was so. And God called the dry land Earth; and the gathering together of the waters called he Seas: and God saw that it was good.'"

ADDRESS TO THE NATION ON THE EXPLOSION OF THE SPACE SHUTTLE *CHALLENGER*

President Ronald Reagan

JANUARY 28, 1986

The Space Shuttle *CHALLENGER* is launched from Kennedy Space Center, Florida. © Jack Novak/SuperStock (2061-528).

Ladies and gentlemen, I'd planned to speak to you tonight to report on the state of the Union, but the events of earlier today have led me to change those plans. Today is a day for mourning and remembering. Nancy and I are pained to the core by the tragedy of the shuttle *Challenger*. We know we share this pain with all of the people of our country. This is truly a national loss.

Nineteen years ago, almost to the day, we lost three astronauts in a terrible accident on the ground. But we've never lost an astronaut in flight; we've never had a tragedy like this. And perhaps we've forgotten the courage it took for the crew of the shuttle. But they, the *Challenger* Seven, were aware of the dangers, but overcame them and did their jobs brilliantly. We mourn seven heroes: Michael Smith, Dick Scobee, Judith Resnik, Ronald McNair, Ellison Onizuka, Gregory Jarvis, and Christa McAuliffe. We mourn their loss as a nation together.

For the families of the seven, we cannot bear, as you do, the full impact of this tragedy. But we feel the loss, and we're thinking about you so very much. Your loved ones were daring and brave, and they had that special grace, that special spirit that says, "Give me a challenge, and

I'll meet it with joy." They had a hunger to explore the universe and discover its truths. They wished to serve, and they did. They served all of us. We've grown used to wonders in this century. It's hard to dazzle us. But for twenty-five years the United States space program has been doing just that. We've grown used to the idea of space, and perhaps we forget that we've only just begun. We're still pioneers. They, the members of the *Challenger* crew, were pioneers.

And I want to say something to the schoolchildren of America who were watching the live coverage of the shuttle's takeoff. I know it is hard to understand, but sometimes painful things like this happen. It's all part of the process of exploration and discovery. It's all part of taking a chance and expanding man's horizons. The future doesn't belong to the faint-hearted; it belongs to the brave. The *Challenger* crew was pulling us into the future, and we'll continue to follow them.

I've always had great faith in and respect for our space program, and what happened today does nothing to diminish it. We don't hide our space program. We don't keep secrets and cover things up. We do it all up front and in public. That's the way freedom is, and we wouldn't change it for a minute. We'll continue our quest in space. There will be more shuttle flights and more shuttle crews and, yes, more volunteers, more civilians, more teachers in space. Nothing ends here; our hopes and our journeys continue. I want to add that I wish I could talk to every man and woman who works for NASA or who worked on this mission and tell them: "Your dedication and professionalism have moved and impressed us for decades. And we know of your anguish. We share it."

There's a coincidence today. On this day 390 years ago, the great explorer Sir Francis Drake died aboard ship off the coast of Panama. In his lifetime the great frontiers were the oceans, and a historian later said, "He lived by the sea, died on it, and was buried in it." Well, today we can say of the *Challenger* crew: Their dedication was, like Drake's, complete.

The crew of the space shuttle *Challenger* honored us by the man-

View of the Pacific Ocean from an overlook on Cape Perpetua, Oregon. © Dennis Frates (LS, se,57t.md).

148

ner in which they lived their lives. We will never forget them, nor the last time we saw them, this morning, as they prepared for their journey and waved goodbye and "slipped the surly bonds of Earth" to "touch the face of God."

Do It Again, Lord

Max Lucado

FOR AMERICA PRAYS, A NATIONAL
PRAYER VIGIL HELD SATURDAY,
SEPTEMBER 14, 2001.

World Trade Center,
September 15, 2001. ©
Greg Martin/SuperStock
(620-725).

Dear Lord, We're still hoping we'll wake up. We're still hoping we'll open a sleepy eye and think, What a horrible dream.

But we won't, will we, Father? What we saw was not a dream. Planes did gouge towers. Flames did consume our fortress. People did perish. It was no dream and, dear Father, we are sad.

There is a ballet dancer who will no longer dance and a doctor who will no longer heal. A church has lost her priest, a classroom is minus a teacher. Cora ran a food pantry. Paige was a counselor and Dana, dearest Father, Dana was only three years old. (Who held her in those final moments?)

We are sad, Father. For as the innocent are buried, our innocence is buried as well. We thought we were safe. Perhaps we should have known better. But we didn't.

And so we come to you. We don't ask you for help; we beg you for it. We don't request it; we implore it. We know what you can do. We've read the accounts. We've pondered the stories and now we plead, Do it again, Lord. Do it again.

Remember Joseph? You rescued him from the pit. You can do the same for us. Do it again, Lord.

Remember the Hebrews in Egypt? You protected their children from the angel of death. We have children, too, Lord. Do it again.

And Sarah? Remember her prayers? You heard them. Joshua? Remember his fears? You inspired him. The women at the tomb? You resurrected their hope. The doubts of Thomas? You took them away. Do it again, Lord. Do it again.

You changed Daniel from a captive into a king's counselor. You took Peter the fisherman and made him Peter an apostle. Because of you, David went from leading sheep to leading armies. Do it again, Lord, for we need counselors today, Lord. We need apostles. We need leaders. Do it again, dear Lord.

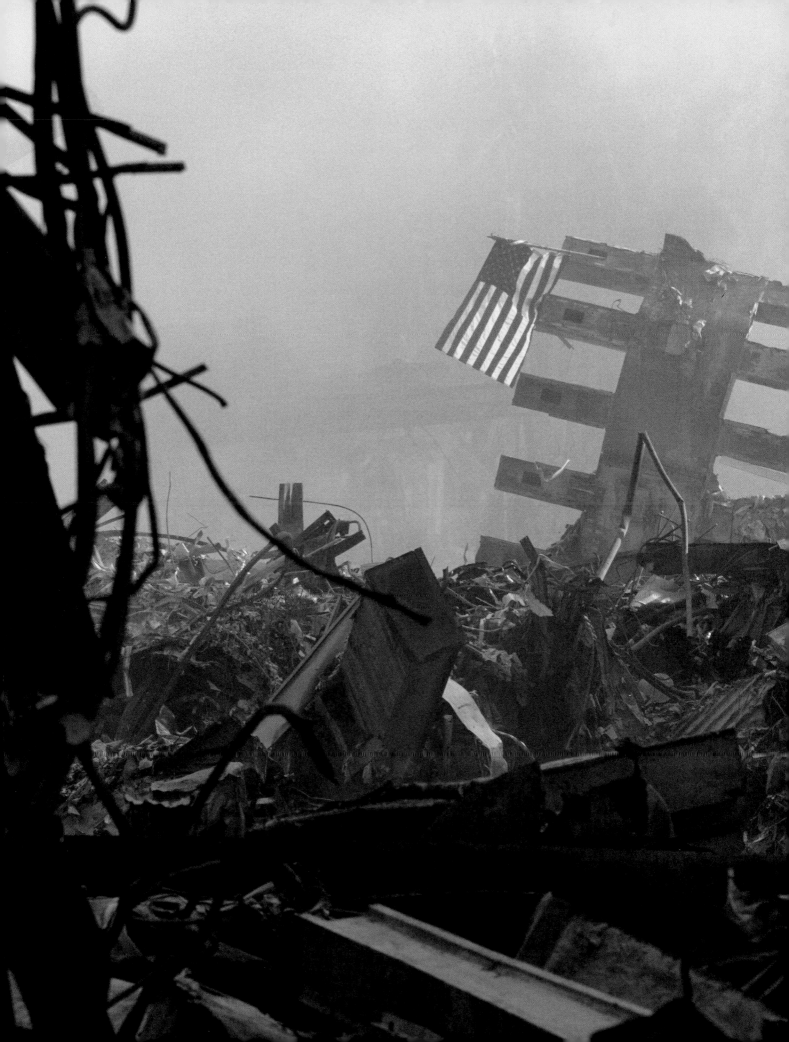

Most of all, do again what you did at Calvary. What we saw here on that Tuesday, you saw there on that Friday. Innocence slaughtered. Goodness murdered. Mothers weeping. Evil dancing. Just as the ash fell on our children, the darkness fell on your Son. Just as our towers were shattered, the very Tower of Eternity was pierced.

And by dusk, heaven's sweetest song was silent, buried behind a rock.

But you did not waver, O Lord. You did not waver. After three days in a dark hole, you rolled the rock and rumbled the earth and turned the darkest Friday into the brightest Sunday. Do it again, Lord. Grant us a September Easter.

We thank you, dear Father, for these hours of unity. Disaster has done what discussion could not. Doctrinal fences have fallen. Republicans are standing with Democrats. Skin colors have been covered by the ash of burning buildings. We thank you for these hours of unity.

And we thank you for these hours of prayer. The Enemy sought to bring us to our knees and succeeded. He had no idea, however, that we would kneel before you. And he has no idea what you can do.

Let your mercy be upon our president, vice president, and their families. Grant to those who lead us wisdom beyond their years and experience. Have mercy upon the souls who have departed and the wounded who remain. Give us grace that we might forgive and faith that we might believe.

And look kindly upon your church. For two thousand years you've used her to heal a hurting world.

Do it again, Lord. Do it again.

Through Christ, Amen.

Mesa arch with morning light reflected on the canyon walls in Canyonlands National Park, Utah. © Dennis Frates (LMM 8099).

152

BE STRONG

MALTBIE D. BABCOCK

Be strong!
We are not here to play, to dream, to drift.
We have hard work to do and loads to lift.
Shun not the struggle, face it: 'tis God's gift.

Be strong!
Say not the days are evil. Who's to blame?
And fold the hands and acquiesce, oh, shame!
Stand up, speak out, and bravely, in God's name.

Be strong!
It matters not how deep entrenched the wrong,
How hard the battle goes, the day how long;
Faint not, fight on! Tomorrow comes the song.

Waves at sunset in Smelt Sands State Park, Oregon.
© Dennis Frates (LSM 12364).

REMARKS BY THE PRESIDENT ON THE LOSS OF SPACE SHUTTLE COLUMBIA

George W. Bush

February 1, 2003

United States Space shuttle COLUMBIA hurtles toward space. © H. Armstrong Roberts (KA-8235-j).

My fellow Americans, this day has brought terrible news and great sadness to our country. At 9:00 A.M. this morning, Mission Control in Houston lost contact with our Space Shuttle *Columbia*. A short time later, debris was seen falling from the skies above Texas. The *Columbia* is lost; there are no survivors.

On board was a crew of seven: Colonel Rick Husband; Lt. Colonel Michael Anderson; Commander Laurel Clark; Captain David Brown; Commander William McCool; Dr. Kalpana Chawla; and Ilan Ramon, a Colonel in the Israeli Air Force. These men and women assumed great risk in the service to all humanity.

In an age when space flight has come to seem almost routine, it is easy to overlook the dangers of travel by rocket, and the difficulties of navigating the fierce outer atmosphere of the Earth. These astronauts knew the dangers, and they faced them willingly, knowing they had a high and noble purpose in life. Because of their courage and daring and idealism, we will miss them all the more.

All Americans today are thinking, as well, of the families of these men and women who have been given this sudden shock and grief. You're not alone. Our entire nation grieves with you. And those you loved will always have the respect and gratitude of this country.

The cause in which they died will continue. Mankind is led into the darkness beyond our world by the inspiration of discovery and the longing to understand. Our journey into space will go on.

In the skies today we saw destruction and tragedy. Yet farther than we can see there is comfort and hope. In the words of the prophet Isaiah, "Lift your eyes and look to the heavens. Who created all these? He who brings out the starry hosts one by one and calls them each by name. Because of his great power and mighty strength, not one of them is missing."

The same Creator who names the stars also knows the names of the seven souls we mourn today. The crew of the shuttle *Columbia* did not return safely to Earth; yet we can pray that all are safely home. May God bless the grieving families, and may God continue to bless America.

Astronaut floating in space. © GoodShoot/SuperStock (1320R-53067).

HIGH FLIGHT

JOHN GILLESPIE MAGEE, JR.

Oh! I have slipped the surly bonds of Earth
And danced the skies on laughter-silvered wings;
Sunward I've climbed, and joined the tumbling mirth
Of sun-split clouds—and done a hundred things
You have not dreamed of—wheeled and soared and swung
High in the sunlit silence. Hov'ring there,
I've chased the shouting wind along, and flung
My eager craft through footless halls of air. . . .

Up, up the long, delirious, burning blue
I've topped the wind-swept heights with easy grace,
Where never lark, or even eagle flew—
And, while with silent, lifting mind I've trod
The high untrespassed sanctity of space,
Put out my hand and touched the face of God.

158

AUTHOR AND TITLE INDEX